Franmarie Kennedy

Thank you for joining me on this Journey to Zero.

Journey to Zero

Journey to Zero

Digital Technology's Quest
for Perfect Health Care

Rubin Pillay, MD, PhD

Copyright © 2023 by Rubin Pillay, MD, PhD.

Library of Congress Control Number:		2023918683
ISBN:	Hardcover	979-8-3694-0864-3
	Softcover	979-8-3694-0863-6
	eBook	979-8-3694-0862-9

All rights reserved. No part of this book may be reproduced or transmitted in any form or by any means, electronic or mechanical, including photocopying, recording, or by any information storage and retrieval system, without permission in writing from the copyright owner.

Any people depicted in stock imagery provided by Getty Images are models, and such images are being used for illustrative purposes only.
Certain stock imagery © Getty Images.

Print information available on the last page.

Rev. date: 11/16/2023

To order additional copies of this book, contact:
Xlibris
844-714-8691
www.Xlibris.com
Orders@Xlibris.com
853772

CONTENTS

Foreword vii
Introduction ix

Zero Cost 1
Zero Harm 17
Zero Wait 42
Zero Stage 65
Zero Exclusion 79
Zero Emission 91
Zero Mistrust 101
Zero Promise Scorecard 111

Conclusion 125

FOREWORD

IN AN ERA punctuated by the lightning-fast evolution of technology and the profound transformations it brings, Dr. Rubin Pillay's "Journey to Zero" stands as a beacon for all healthcare professionals, technologists, and patients. This insightful tome delves deep into the realm where cutting-edge digital technologies and the timeless pursuit of flawless healthcare converge.

"Journey to Zero" is not just a book; it's a manifesto that challenges the status quo of healthcare. Dr. Pillay, with his astute observations and unparalleled expertise, presents a compelling vision of a future where errors are not just reduced but eradicated. Where technology doesn't just assist but seamlessly integrates with every facet of patient care, ensuring that the age-old goal of 'do no harm' is upheld to its utmost potential.

As you flip through these pages, you'll be introduced to a world where Artificial Intelligence, Big Data, and other digital tools are not mere buzzwords but vital instruments that bridge the chasm between today's healthcare challenges and tomorrow's solutions. Dr. Pillay masterfully showcases how these technologies can be harnessed to transform the very fabric of patient care, making it more personalized, efficient, and above all, safe.

But this book is not just about technology. It's about the human spirit, the relentless pursuit of perfection, and the belief that we can always do better. It's about the countless healthcare professionals who, day in and day out, strive to provide the best care possible and the patients who entrust them with their well-being.

In "Journey to Zero," Dr. Pillay beckons us all to join this transformative journey. A journey that is not just about improving healthcare but reimagining it. A journey where the endpoint is not just better care but perfect care.

As you embark on this enlightening expedition with Dr. Pillay, be prepared to be challenged, inspired, and above all, hopeful. Hopeful for a future where digital technology and human endeavor come together in harmony to create a healthcare system that truly lives up to its promise.

Welcome to the journey. The journey to zero.

- Selwyn M. Vickers, MD, FACS
President and CEO
Memorial Sloan Kettering Cancer Center
New York

INTRODUCTION

OVER THE PAST several decades, the development and accelerated advancement of digital technology has prompted change across virtually all aspects of human endeavor. The health care industry is undergoing a major transformation. Digital technologies are giving people greater access to health information and resources, enabling them to improve every aspect of health care from prevention and diagnosis to treatment and management. These technologies have the potential to revolutionize health care, making it more accessible, affordable, and effective. With 10 billion people—that's the global population projected by 2050, and with many enjoying longer lives—the services required by health care systems will have to adapt and grow. Digital technologies offer tremendous potential for shifting from traditional medical routines to remote medicine and transforming our ability to manage health and independence in aging populations. No one can be certain how the industry will evolve, but with new challenges come exciting solutions.

The convergence of three main drivers is the catalyst for many health care organizations to start their digital transformation, with the goal to create more value for patients along the continuum of care, including the following:

- cost pressures, demographics, and the rise of chronic diseases
- a digital, empowered, "connected" patient who shares valuable data with the wider community
- the emergence of digital technology and advanced medical devices, sensors, and wearables for extended monitoring and prevention and more fact-based care decisions

Meet Alex. He's forty-two years old and seemingly healthy. When walking his dog, Alex is alerted about a deviation in his health condition by his wearable device and advised to see a doctor. He schedules an appointment with his family physician in one click using his smartphone. The physician reviews Alex's patient history, including the most recent information from his wearable device, performs an examination, and advises Alex to see a cardiologist. Using a registry of ranking specialists, Alex receives recommendations based on his personal preference and schedules an appointment. By giving the cardiologist access to Alex's patient history, Alex enables her to review all relevant information prior to the appointment. After her examination, the specialist adds her diagnosis to Alex's patient history. Comparing Alex's patient profile against a large set of patients with the same disease and similar health profiles, she can predict that the standard surgery for this disease would be risky for Alex. The analysis shows that for Alex's specific case, a certain drug can be expected to provide the best outcomes. Because Alex has given his consent to mapping his profile against ongoing clinical studies, he is matched to a clinical trial that has shown positive results and fewer side effects than with current drugs on the market. Alex decides to enroll in the clinical trial to benefit from the new drug and to contribute his data to the research study. As part of the trial, Alex downloads an app to track specific health parameters. He uses his monitoring device to manage his physical activity and resumes life as before, knowing that he will be notified if anything urgent arises. Meanwhile, the smart care team consisting of doctors and supporting professionals remotely monitor Alex's progress in real time through the information provided by his wearable device. They use this information to advise him on his daily plan, if necessary, and motivate Alex to continue on his prescriptions and follow his health plan. Alex has also given his consent for his data to be used by researchers in different organizations for the creation of new drugs and the adaption of drugs in order to help improve the lives of patients just like him.

This is the patient journey in the digital age! Welcome to *Journey to Zero: Digital Technology's Quest for Perfect Health Care*. This book is a voyage of exploration, envisioning the transformative potential of digital technology to reshape the health care landscape and draw us closer to an ideal of perfect health care. The term "perfect health care" may seem audacious, even utopian. It evokes an image of a world where disease is predicted before onset, where treatment is accurate, timely, and causes no harm, where care is accessible and affordable for all, regardless of their social, economic, or geographic backgrounds, and where patient and provider can engage in health care delivery with utmost trust and minimal environmental impact.

In pursuit of this ideal, we propose seven ambitious goals, embodied in the concept of seven "zeros": zero cost care, zero harm, zero wait, zero stage, zero excluded, zero mistrust, and zero emission. Each "zero" presents its unique challenges and opportunities, serving as a guidepost in our journey toward perfect health care.

This journey isn't linear or straightforward. It is filled with complex intersections of medical practice, technology, policy, ethics, and human behavior. Our exploration is not limited to presenting an optimistic view of technology's potential but extends to an honest examination of its challenges, including the digital divide, privacy concerns, and ecological footprint of our technological progress.

In the forthcoming chapters, we delve into each of the seven "zeros," discussing their implications, showcasing real-world examples, and presenting forward-looking strategies. We explore the role of various stakeholders, including technology innovators, health care providers, policymakers, and patients, in realizing these goals. Whether you are a health care professional, technology enthusiast, policymaker, or patient interested in the future of health care, this book is a map for you. It aims to provide insights, ignite discussions, and inspire actions toward a future where digital technology is not just a tool but a trusted ally in our quest for perfect health care.

So as we embark on this journey to zero, let us challenge our assumptions, spark our imaginations, and dare to envision a future where perfect health care isn't a mere aspiration but a reality within our grasp. Welcome aboard.

ZERO COST

AS WE NAVIGATE into the future of health care, a new frontier is being ushered in by digital health technology. One of the most ambitious targets of this revolution is to achieve a zero marginal cost scenario, where the cost of providing health care to an additional patient becomes almost negligible. While this might seem utopian, digital health technology makes it a conceivable reality. This economic paradigm, based on the principle that certain goods and services can be produced and distributed at effectively zero marginal cost, has triggered a profound transformation of traditional business models and has far-reaching implications for society, the environment, and the global economy. The zero marginal cost concept is not entirely new in economic theory. The theory suggests that in an ideal production setup, costs decrease as output increases, resulting in marginal cost—the cost to produce an additional unit—trending toward zero. This concept has become increasingly practical due to the advent of the internet and the digital revolution, leading to the emergence of the zero marginal cost economy. Information goods, such as music, movies, books, software, and even education and news, can be digitally duplicated and distributed at virtually zero marginal cost, once the initial creation or setup costs are covered. In addition, certain physical goods can also experience low marginal costs due to advancements in automation and manufacturing technologies.

Peter Diamandis,[1] a renowned entrepreneur, futurist, and visionary, has made significant contributions to the concept of demonetization in the context of digital technology. As the cofounder of Singularity University and the XPRIZE Foundation, Diamandis has been at the forefront of fostering innovation and accelerating transformative technologies. His work highlights the profound impact that the

---

[1] https://www.diamandis.com/blog/demonetized-cost-of-living.

demonetization of digital technology can have on various industries and society as a whole. Demonetization refers to the process by which technology disrupts established industries, making goods and services that were once expensive or scarce increasingly affordable or even free. Rapid technological advancements, particularly in the digital realm, are driving this process of demonetization, leading to widespread accessibility, democratization, and abundance. There are several key factors contributing to demonetization, including the following:

- Moore's law and computing power. Moore's law, which states that computing power doubles approximately every two years, has led to the exponential growth of digital capabilities. The increasing power of computing devices at reduced costs has catalyzed the demonetization of various technologies, making them more accessible to a broader population.
- connectivity and global access. The proliferation of the internet and advancements in telecommunications have connected people across the globe. Digital connectivity has created new opportunities for innovation, collaboration, and access to knowledge. It has enabled the sharing of ideas, solutions, and resources on a scale never seen before, further driving the demonetization of digital technologies.
- open-source movement. The open-source movement, championed by communities of developers, has revolutionized software and technology. Open-source projects make code and intellectual property freely available, allowing for collaboration, customization, and accelerated innovation. This collaborative approach has significantly contributed to the demonetization of software, as well as the democratization of access to technology.

So put simply, demonetization means the ability of technology to take a product or service that was previously expensive and make it substantially cheaper or potentially free. It means removing money from the equation. Demonetization in the digital realm has transformative implications for society. As technology continues to advance, it has the potential to unlock a world of abundance, democratize access to goods and services, and address global challenges. The widespread availability and affordability of digital technology, driven by demonetization, enable individuals and communities to connect.

Consider photography. In the Kodak years, photography was expensive. You paid for the camera, for the film, for developing the film, and so on. Today, during the megapixel era, the camera is free in your phone—no film, no developing. Completely demonetized.

Consider information/research. In years past, collecting obscure data was hard, expensive in time if you did it yourself, or expensive in money if you hired researchers. Today, during the Google era, it's free, and the quality is a thousand times better. Access to information, data, and research is fully demonetized.

Consider live video or phone calls. They are demonetized by Skype, Google Hangouts, and the list goes on.

- Craigslist demonetized classifieds.
- iTunes demonetized the music industry.
- Uber demonetized transportation.
- Airbnb demonetized hotels.
- Amazon demonetized bookstores.

People with a smartphone today can access tools that would have cost thousands a few decades ago. Twenty years ago, most well-off US citizens owned a camera, a video camera, a CD player, a stereo, a video game console, a cell phone, a watch, an alarm clock, a set of encyclopedias, a world atlas, a Thomas guide, and a whole bunch of other assets that easily add up to more than $900,000. Today, all of these things are free on your smartphone.

While having a pocket-sized phone and camera is a nice luxury, today's smartphones perform a range of tasks that until recently would have been deemed unimaginable. With more computing power than the computer aboard the *Apollo 11* spaceship, smartphones now do everything from shopping and managing finances to translating foreign languages and helping us navigate virtually anywhere on the planet.

Smartphones will also make the world healthier at zero cost. More than 5 billion people around the world have access to mobile phones but not to a physician. We can do what a $100,000 device can do on a mobile phone, with ten times better magnification than using just the naked eye, raising diagnostic accuracy significantly. High-quality care can now be augmented with deep technology and delivered via a smartphone.

The same devices used to take selfies are being repurposed for quick access to information needed for monitoring patient health. A fingertip pressed against a phone's camera lens can measure a heart rate—for free! The microphone, kept by the bedside, can screen for sleep apnea—for free! And in the best of this new world, the data is conveyed remotely to a medical professional for the convenience and comfort of the patient—all without the need for costly hardware. Smartphones come packed with sensors capable of monitoring a patient's vital signs. They can help assess people for concussions, watch for atrial fibrillation, and conduct mental health wellness checks, to name a few nascent applications. Eager companies and researchers are tapping into phones' built-in cameras and light sensors, microphones, accelerometers, which detect body movements; gyroscopes, and even speakers. The apps then use artificial intelligence software to analyze the collected sights and sounds to create an easy connection between patients and physicians. In 2021 more than 350,000 digital health products were available in app stores, according to a Grand View Research report.[2] The power of this convergence between AI and smartphone technology is likely to be immense. AI doctors could provide far better and cheaper (and even free) health care for billions of people, particularly for those who currently receive no health care at all. Thanks to learning algorithms and biometric sensors, a poor villager in an underdeveloped country might come to enjoy far better health care via her smartphone than the richest person in the world gets today from the most advanced urban hospital—for free!

---

[2] https://www.grandviewresearch.com/industry-analysis/mhealth-app-market.

Big tech companies such as Google[3] have heavily invested in the area, catering to clinicians and in-home caregivers as well as consumers. Currently, Google Fit app users can check their heart rate by placing their finger on the rear-facing camera lens or track their breathing rate using the front-facing camera—for free! Google's research uses machine learning and computer vision, a field within AI based on information from visual inputs such as videos or images. So instead of using a blood pressure cuff, for example, the algorithm can interpret slight visual changes to the body that serve as proxies and biosignals for blood pressure—for free! Google is also investigating the effectiveness of its smartphone's built-in microphone for detecting heartbeats and murmurs and using the camera to preserve eyesight by screening for diabetic eye disease—for free! They also use a smart device's speaker to bounce inaudible pulses off a patient's body to identify movement and monitor breathing. In a recent announcement, Google revealed a groundbreaking development. Using Google's AI, cardiovascular events can now be predicted through an eye scan, signifying a potential departure from traditional diagnostic methods like CT scans, MRIs, and x-rays—for free!

Two billion people around the world have skin, hair, and nail conditions. Google's DermAssist allows you to use your phone or computer to upload three photos of your skin condition and answer a few questions. Using what it has learned from millions of skin-related images, DermAssist then looks for signs of various skin conditions in your submitted photos and information. You receive results within a minute, and in a matter of seconds, DermAssist provides you with a list of possible matching skin conditions and helpful information about each—for free! A study in *Nature* in 2020[4] confirmed that on cleaned data for selected lesions, AI is as good as or even superior to human experts in image-based diagnosis. Which is a good thing, considering that there's a constant shortage of dermatologists, especially in rural areas. Therefore, the boom is understandable, as you can easily detect if you have a

---

[3] https://health.google/.
[4] https://www.nature.com/articles/s41591-020-0942-0.

skin problem. Smartphones coupled with super-fast internet connection make it easy to check images against databases, send pictures or footage anywhere, understand self-surveillance solutions, and receive disease guides, so educational apps as well as telehealth platforms have appeared naturally in dermatology. Pioneering the technology on the market, SkinVision started working on the technology in 2012. DermAssist, another company, announced that it received the European CE mark for its smartphone-based dermatology AI component. Australian-based medical investment firm Advanced Human Imaging (AHI) bought the Canadian startup Triage to enter the market. Its DermaScan app is capable of screening 588 skin conditions in 134 categories with a smartphone. As of 2022, there were 632 dermatology apps available on the Google Play Store and Apple App Store. Ninety-four percent were free while the most expensive price for an in-person dermatologic consult was $399.96![5]

Binah.ai's[6] video-based solution provides medical-grade vital signs measurements—heart rate, heart rate variability, mental stress level, oxygen saturation, respiration rate, and more—within two minutes via a video of the patient's upper cheek taken with a smartphone, tablet, or laptop. The signal processing and AI technology compensate for motion and imperfect lighting and support any age, gender, and skin color. It can even detect subtle changes that might otherwise go unnoticed.

---

[5] https://www.ncbi.nlm.nih.gov/pmc/articles/PMC8949477/.
[6] https://www.binah.ai/.

Video-Based Vital Signs Monitoring[7]

Anura[8] is the world's first and most comprehensive video-based health and wellness measurement app. The application uses the camera on your mobile device to assess your general wellness, providing medical grade measurements using data gathered from a thirty-second video selfie. Anura is the creator of the world's first contactless blood pressure measurement technology. The company's patented technology can measure thirtysomething health and wellness parameters using Transdermal Optical Imaging (TOI™)—for free!

With the microphone, Canary Speech[9] uses the same underlying technology as Amazon's Alexa to analyze patients' voices for mental health conditions. Their patented vocal biomarker technology model's acoustic and linguistic features return analysis using just twenty seconds of conversational speech. Canary detects respiratory conditions, dementia and Alzheimer's, stress, mood, and energy levels ahead of traditional clinical screening and before observable symptoms—for free!

---

[7] https://www.binah.ai/technology/.
[8] https://www.nuralogix.ai/anura/.
[9] https://canaryspeech.com/.

Australia-based ResApp Health[10] got FDA clearance in 2022 for an iPhone app that screens for respiratory diseases. This powerful platform for respiratory disease diagnosis and management only requires the sound of the patient's cough or breathing and does not require physical contact. With the high-quality microphones in today's smartphones the platform can be delivered without the need for additional hardware. Their SleepCheckRx program identifies obstructive sleep apnea by listening to overnight breathing and snoring sounds. Physicians currently test sleep apnea in a sleep lab where attendants use sensors to monitor a patient's heart, lungs, brain activity, breathing patterns, arm and leg movements, and blood-oxygen saturation levels. When patients use SleepCheckRx, they place their smartphone with the app running on a table next to the bed at home. Sleeping at home without sensors stuck all over your body sounds like a much more comfortable night than in a lab. The national average for a sleep study at a hospital or sleep center is $3,075. SleepCheckRx is free!

Similarly Cordio Medical's HearO technology[11] can sense fluid accumulation related to congestive heart failure through a patient's speech and send an alert. This is the only noninvasive, easy-to-use, medical-grade, CHF-monitoring device that offers patients and caretakers peace of mind and a true sense of control—for free!

These are just some examples of how the chain reaction of digitalization (conversion of biology to ones and zeros) and dematerialization (medical devices that are bulky now fit into your smartphone) drive the demonetization (becomes cheaper, ultimately free!) of health care. Truly leveraging the power of technology and smartphones to deliver far-reaching and cost-efficient high-quality care to literally everyone in the world will require innovative thinking and the willingness of both patients and doctors to adopt a paradigm shift. But it will be worth it. Enabling people to access that level of care from their smartphone will literally make the world a healthier and better place by enabling everyone to share in the benefits of early

---

[10] https://www.resapphealth.com.au/.
[11] https://www.cordio-med.com/.

and often health care. Investing in a company that capitalizes on this opportunity might very well create the ultimate "doing well and doing good" investment. While the approach is intuitive and the benefits and business opportunities massive, there are nonetheless many regulatory complexities and technological challenges to develop a user-friendly product that delivers the impeccable quality necessary to properly care for patients.

Making these solutions available to consumers at zero cost is a challenging task as there are always costs associated with providing any kind of service. However, there are certain strategies that innovators and entrepreneurs can consider to minimize costs or offer a service free. Here are a few approaches:

- advertising and sponsorships. Generate revenue by partnering with advertisers or sponsors who are willing to support your service financially in exchange for exposure or access to your user base. This can help offset the costs and potentially make the service free for users.
- personalized advertisements and recommendations. If the wearable or app has access to user preferences, lifestyle choices, or health data, it can be used to deliver personalized advertisements or recommendations. Advertisers or health-related product/service providers may be interested in targeting specific user segments based on their data profiles, leading to potential monetization opportunities.
- freemium model. Offer a basic version of your service for free while charging for advanced features or additional services. This approach allows you to attract a large user base with the free offering while monetizing certain aspects of the service to cover costs.
- aggregated and anonymized data sales. One approach is to aggregate and anonymize the collected data from wearables or apps, removing any personally identifiable information. This aggregated data can then be sold to researchers, health care organizations, or pharmaceutical companies for various

purposes, such as population health analysis, drug development, or market research.
- data analytics and insights. Utilize the collected data to derive valuable insights and analytics. These insights can be packaged and offered as a service to health care providers, insurance companies, or other stakeholders in the health care industry. For example, offering data-driven reports on population health trends, patient behavior patterns, or personalized recommendations based on the data.
- market research and surveys. Leverage the data collected to conduct market research or surveys on specific health-related topics. This data can be sold to companies or organizations interested in understanding consumer preferences, behavior, or trends.
- crowdfunding or grants. Explore crowdfunding platforms or apply for grants to gather funds for your service. By presenting your idea to the public or specific organizations, you may be able to secure financial support to cover the costs and offer the service at a reduced or zero cost.
- subsidization or partnerships. Seek partnerships with organizations or entities that have a shared interest in the service you provide. They may be willing to subsidize or cover a portion of the costs to ensure the service remains affordable or free for users.
- open source and community support. Consider adopting an open-source model where the community contributes to the development and maintenance of the service. This can help reduce costs as volunteers or contributors assist in the service's upkeep.
- government funding or nonprofit status. Investigate potential government grants or funding programs aimed at supporting initiatives aligned with social, educational, or public service goals. Additionally, establishing your service as a nonprofit organization may provide access to certain resources, grants, or tax benefits.

It's important to note that even if you manage to minimize or cover costs, sustaining a service in the long term often requires a stable financial model. Exploring revenue streams beyond the direct cost of the service itself can be crucial for ongoing viability. It is important to ensure that any data monetization approach adheres to privacy regulations, ethical guidelines, and obtains explicit consent from users regarding data usage. Transparency and data security are key considerations when exploring these strategies to build trust with users and maintain compliance with relevant regulations.

In addition to digitization that is helping us drive costs to zero, the commoditization of medical technology presents an opportunity to revolutionize health services, potentially making them free for the masses. The concept of commoditization, traditionally associated with tangible goods, has extended its reach to the health care industry, transforming the way services are viewed, valued, and delivered. It refers to the transformation of medical knowledge, services, and technologies into interchangeable, mass-market products and implies the standardization of services previously considered unique, specialized, and the sole purview of the medical profession. The over-the-counter pregnancy tests are a good example of a commoditized medical technology. They are widely available, relatively inexpensive, and their technology is largely standardized. It's available on Amazon for approximately $3 a test! (But it is upward of $100 at urgent cares or primary care clinics.) The convergence of the internet, connectivity, and smartphone technology means that medical knowledge is also always available on connected devices to all, free.

The Commoditization of Medical Knowledge

The convergence of exponential technologies in medical science, software, hardware, and communications is now also giving patients unprecedented access to the tools to not only participate in but also direct their own care. The commoditization of medical technology is driving the elevation of patients from consumers to prosumers—patients who produce their own care, at marginal costs approaching zero.

Glucometers and home blood pressure monitors, devices for monitoring blood sugar levels and blood pressure home, have also become commoditized. They provide essential support for people with diabetes and hypertension and have become so standardized that mainly price rather than brand or additional features differentiates them. Both can be purchased for under $50, so breakeven is approximately one to two copays. Thereafter, glucose and BP monitoring are free (except for the cost of glucostrips). Note that these two technologies have also been totally dematerialized and demonetized and can be available just through the download of an app. See above.

AliveCor's KardiaMobile EKG[12] monitor is a personal device designed to provide some of the same information as an advanced version that your doctor might use. The basic device costs $89 and the advanced 6Lead costs $139. On average, an EKG costs $205 at urgent care facilities; however, prices can range from about $175 to $299. At a hospital, the national average cost is around $1,500. The breakeven on the advanced Kardia is equivalent to about two to three copays, and thereafter every following EKG is free! Great if you require regular monitoring.

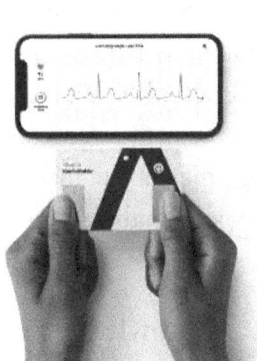

KardiaMobile® 6L

The world's only 6-lead personal EKG. Clinically validated to give you a more detailed view of your heart.

Kardiamobile Card[13]

---

[12] https://store.kardia.com/.

[13] https://www.alivecor.com/products.

According to the American Optometry Association, as an adult, you should go to the eye doctor for an eye exam at least every two years. If your doctor sees health concerns or vision changes, they may ask to see you every year. Even adults without vision concerns should have a routine exam every few years. If you are visiting an eye doctor for the first time, an initial patient visit with an exam could be around $250. EyeQue[14] has commoditized this service with their Vision Monitoring Kit that retails for $160.00. This measures your visual acuity, color contrast, nearsightedness, farsightedness, astigmatism, and more and also generates a prescription. The breakeven on this solution is less than the cost of one visit, and thereafter, eye testing becomes free for the family!

Eyecue Smartphone Vision Test[15]

Aidar Health[16] has developed an FDA-approved equivalent of a medical tricorder, which is an iPhone-sized device, the MouthLab, that the patient puts into their mouth, breathes normally, and positions their hands on the device as instructed. The MouthLab will record temperature, respiration rate, pulse rate, blood pressure, respiration

---

[14] https://store.eyeque.com/vision-monitoring-kit.html.
[15] https://www.eyeque.com/.
[16] https://www.aidar.com/.

pattern, heart rate, heart rate variability, ECG, spirometry (i.e., lung function), and oxygen saturation. Data is collected from sensors across the device from saliva, breathing, hand pulse, and lips to read the body's parameters. In a world where digital and remote care has become the new norm thanks to the COVID-19 pandemic, physicians have often had to go off what their patients say, which is a good starting point but not sufficient for long-term care. Although tests and labs are done eventually, there hasn't been an efficient way to track a patient's vitals at home. Aidar has created a new paradigm for personalized care at home, reimagining today's standards for disease management, digital medicine, and aging in place. The MouthLab will be commercially available for $200, and breakeven is the price of one primary care visit; thereafter, all assessments and evaluations are free—for the household!

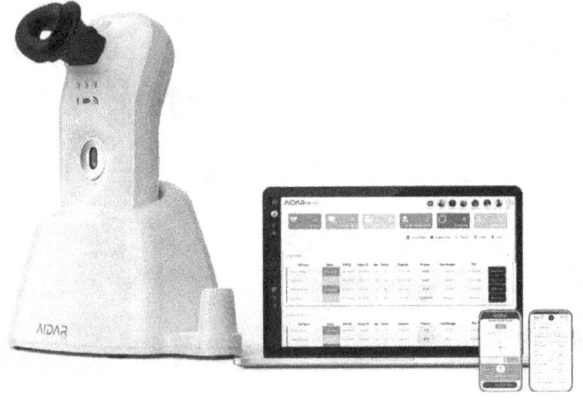

The Aidar MouthLab[17]

These are just some examples of how medical technology can drive down the costs of health by commoditization. The key for founders and startups operating in this space is to craft business models that enable their products to be available on the open market and accessible to all, and *not* focus on embedding solutions in health care systems. Society will never reap the cost benefits that these disruptive technologies offer

---

[17] https://www.aidar.com/.

due to the inefficient business models and cost structures of health care systems. Hospitals and healthy systems are where innovation goes to die! Similarly society would not have reaped the cost, geographic access, and efficiency gains of Uber, if the platform had been sold to the taxi industry!

Commoditization can also foster innovation and competition. As services become more price transparent, providers are compelled to seek novel ways to differentiate themselves, potentially driving quality improvements and technological advancements. The rise of telemedicine, mobile health apps, and online appointment platforms are just some examples of innovation stemming from commoditized health care.

The continued growth in Health Savings Accounts (HSAs) and Flexible Spending Accounts (FSAs)[18]—tax-deductible personal savings account you can set up to pay certain health care costs—will propel the growth of the commoditized medical technology market. The ability of consumers to exercise choice in products and services and pay for these using FSAs and HSAs will drive this trend.

As we conclude this chapter on how digital technology and commoditization enable zero cost health care, we stand at a pivotal point in the evolution of health care. The fusion of digital technology and health care has the potential to fundamentally alter the way health care is accessed, delivered, and experienced.

Commoditization of health care technology can democratize health care, making it more affordable and accessible. We've discussed various forms of digital technologies—from telemedicine and AI-driven diagnostics to digital therapeutics and mobile health applications—and examined how their commoditization could lead to substantial cost reductions. However, as we have also seen, achieving zero cost care is not without challenges.

Despite the potential benefits, the transition to commoditized digital health services must be navigated carefully. Equity, quality, and safety must remain paramount. Health care cannot be simplified

---

[18] https://www.devenir.com/research/2022-year-end-devenir-hsa-research-report/.

to mere transactions; the personal and human aspects of care must be retained. Additionally, concerns around data privacy and security should be duly addressed.

Moreover, it is essential to remember that digital technology and commoditization are tools that can help facilitate zero cost care, but they aren't the panacea. A multipronged approach that includes policy interventions, strategic innovation, and broad-scale collaboration is needed. Investments in health care infrastructure, digital literacy, and robust regulatory frameworks are equally important in achieving the ideal of zero cost health care.

Digital technology and commoditization provide us with a powerful opportunity to rethink and redefine the economics of health care. They offer a pathway to making zero cost care, once a far-fetched dream, a tangible possibility. As we continue our journey to zero, let's harness these tools with intention, creativity, and a deep commitment to inclusivity and fairness. The vision of perfect health care is one where no one is denied care because of cost, and with the careful application of digital technology, we inch closer to making that vision a reality.

ZERO HARM

AS WE EMBARK on this chapter of our journey to zero, we navigate toward a crucial beacon: zero harm. In an ideal health care system, treatments are not just effective but safe, and care delivery processes do not result in adverse events. The goal of zero harm resonates with the ancient medical adage "Primum non nocere." (First, do no harm.) Despite our best intentions and efforts, the reality of modern health care is fraught with instances of unintended harm. Medical errors, hospital-acquired infections, medication mishaps, and misdiagnoses are just some of the ways patients can be inadvertently harmed in the process of seeking care.

Digital health technology promises a sea of change in this landscape. With advanced analytics, artificial intelligence, telemedicine, electronic health records, and a host of other tools, we have the potential to enhance patient safety like never before. The goal of zero harm can move from being an aspiration to an achievable target. In this chapter, we will explore how digital technology can be harnessed to prevent harm in health care. We will delve into examples of successful implementations and the lessons learned. We will discuss the potential challenges that lie ahead and strategies to overcome them. From detecting anomalies in real time to ensuring the right patient receives the right treatment at the right time, we will see how digital health technology can play a crucial role in ensuring patient safety. As we proceed, we must remember that technology is an enabler, not a replacement, for human judgment and expertise. Therefore, we must aim for a synergistic relationship between health care professionals and technology.

The journey to zero harm is a complex and challenging one, but with the right application of digital technology, it's a goal within our reach. It's time to harness the potential of digital health and make zero harm not just an ideal but a reality in health care. Let's explore this exciting frontier together.

Every year, millions of patients suffer injuries or die because of unsafe and poor-quality health care. Many medical practices and risks associated with health care are emerging as major challenges for patient safety and contribute significantly to the burden of harm due to unsafe care. The occurrence of adverse events due to unsafe care is likely one of the ten leading causes of death and disability in the world.[19] In high-income countries, it is estimated that one in every ten patients is harmed while receiving hospital care.[20] The harm can be caused by a range of adverse events, with nearly 50 percent of them being preventable.[21] Each year, 134 million adverse events occur in hospitals in low- and middle-income countries (LMICs) due to unsafe care, resulting in 2.6 million deaths.[22] Another study has estimated that around two-thirds of all adverse events resulting from unsafe care, and the years lost to disability and death (known as disability-adjusted life years or DALYs) occur in LMICs.[23]

---

[19] Jha, A. K. Presentation at "Patient Safety—A Grand Challenge for Healthcare Professionals and Policymakers Alike," a Roundtable at the Grand Challenges Meeting of the Bill & Melinda Gates Foundation, October 18, 2018, (https://globalhealth.harvard.edu/qualitypowerpoint.

[20] Slawomirski L., Auraaen A., Klazinga N. "The Economics of Patient Safety: Strengthening a Value-Based Approach to Reducing Patient Harm at National Level." Paris: OECD, 2017 (http://www.oecd.org/els/health-systems/The-economics-of-patient-safety-March-2017.

[21] Singh, H., Meyer, A. N., Thomas, E. J. "The Frequency of Diagnostic Errors in Outpatient Care: Estimations from Three Large Observational Studies Involving US Adult Populations." *BMJ Qual Saf.* 2014;23(9):727–31, https://doi.org/10.1136/bmjqs-2013-002627 https://www.ncbi.nlm.nih.gov/pubmed/24742777.

[22] National Academies of Sciences, Engineering, and Medicine. "Crossing the Global Quality Chasm: Improving Health Care Worldwide." Washington, DC: The National Academies Press, 2018, (https://www.nap.edu/catalog/25152/crossing-the-global-quality-chasm-improving-health-care-worldwide).

[23] Jha, A. K., Larizgoitia, I., Audera-Lopez, C., Prasopa-Plaizier, N., Waters, H., Bates, D. W. "The Global Burden of Unsafe Medical Care: Analytic Modelling of Observational Studies." *BMJ Qual Saf*, published online first: September 18, 2013, https://doi.org/10.1136/bmjqs-2012-001748, https://www.ncbi.nlm.nih.gov/pubmed/24048616.

Globally, as many as four in ten patients are harmed in primary and outpatient health care. Up to 80 percent of harm is preventable. The most detrimental errors are related to diagnosis, prescription, and the use of medicines.[24] In OECD countries, 15 percent of total hospital activity and expenditure is a direct result of adverse events.[25]

Digital health is revolutionizing the health care sector, introducing innovative solutions that not only enhance the delivery of care but also play a crucial role in improving patient safety and reducing harm. In this chapter, we will delve into the ways digital health technologies can be leveraged to minimize medical errors, increase treatment efficiency, and ensure safer health care outcomes—in short, cause zero harm!

Digital health encompasses various technology-driven tools like electronic health records (EHRs), telemedicine, artificial intelligence (AI), wearable devices, and mobile health applications. By providing real-time, accurate health information and enabling efficient care processes, these tools are playing a significant role in enhancing patient safety. EHRs have replaced traditional paper records in many health care facilities, improving the accuracy, accessibility, and organization of patient information. They provide health care professionals with comprehensive patient histories, reducing the likelihood of errors stemming from incomplete or inaccessible information. EHRs also support decision-making through features like alert systems for drug interactions and automatic risk stratification and escalation. Automated flags and alerts improve clinical decision-making. One such example is the detection of abnormal kidney functions from laboratory investigations and highlighting more "kidney-friendly" alternatives to the clinician during prescription. Automation of workflows reduces

---

[24] Slawomirski L., Auraaen A., Klazinga N. "The Economics of Patient Safety in Primary and Ambulatory Care: Flying Blind." Paris: OECD; 2018 (http://www.oecd.org/health/health-systems/The-Economics-of-Patient-Safety-in-Primary-and-Ambulatory-Care-April2018.pd.

[25] Slawomirski L., Auraaen A., Klazinga N. "The Economics of Patient Safety: Strengthening a Value-Based Approach to Reducing Patient Harm at National Level." Paris: OECD; 2017 (http://www.oecd.org/els/health-systems/The-economics-of-patient-safety-March-2017.pdf.

the cognitive load on the clinician by programming certain crucial steps according to the agreed clinical protocol. A good example is monitoring certain medications that are necessary for treatment but known to have adverse effects for some individuals. These medications are prescribed under a monitoring protocol that usually involves a laboratory test after a month of starting the medication. In this case, automated scripts schedule the right investigation within the most appropriate duration after starting the treatment, with no additional human intervention.

Medication errors are a leading cause of injury and avoidable harm in health care systems. Globally, the cost associated with medication errors has been estimated at $42 billion annually. Bar Code Medication Administration Systems (BCMA) use barcodes to verify that the "Five Rights" of medication administration are followed: the right patient, right drug, right dose, right route, and right time. This technology reduces the likelihood of medication administration errors, a common source of patient harm. To prevent medication errors, hospitals are using AI algorithms to scan EMRs for any signs or patterns that an error has occurred, such as a patient becoming oversedated. The algorithms can also notify clinicians of potential harm in real time by identifying changes in lab results that could be out of place. For example, a tool has identified patients who were on three or more medications that could be toxic to their kidneys, which allowed pharmacists to notify physicians of potential risks and make changes as needed.

One telemedicine program that connected pediatric critical care physicians at a large academic medical center with eight rural emergency departments caring for seriously ill or injured children in underserved areas of northern California demonstrated significantly fewer medication errors compared with patients receiving telephone consultations or no consultations (3.4 percent for telemedicine program versus 10.8 percent for telephone consultations versus 12.5 percent for no consultations). Furthermore, AI-powered clinical decision support systems can detect potential drug interactions or allergic reactions, alerting physicians and preventing harmful errors.

Pill Connect[26] is another smart solution designed to tackle the medication adherence and safety issue. Created by Elucid Health, this smart pill bottle is connected to a smartphone app and dispenses the pills in accordance with the patient's dosage and regimen. The app notifies the patient when it's time to take the drug and then informs their doctor once the pill has been dispensed. To prevent the patient from taking an accidental double dose, the bottle remains locked outside of the stipulated dosage times.

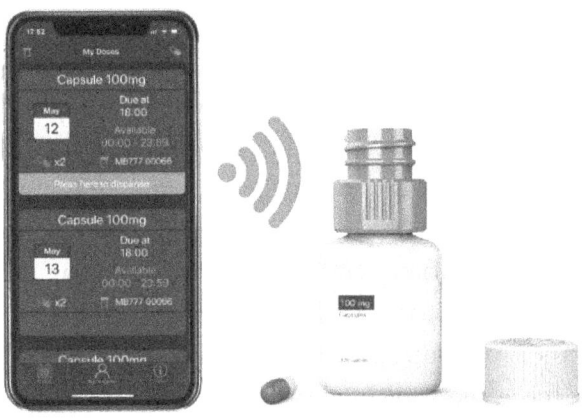

Pill Connect[26]

Besides improving drug delivery, smart pills could also be used to enhance diagnosis and further treatment. SmarTab[27] is a new smart capsule that uses artificial intelligence to diagnose gastrointestinal cancers and bleeding problems faster and with more precision than existing diagnostic methods. Currently in the prototype development stage, the SmarTab is equipped with miniature wireless biosensors capable of detecting and analyzing biomarkers that indicate the presence of disease. Using the on-board multispectral sensor array, the capsule can determine hemoglobin concentrations and blood-oxygen saturation,

---

[26] https://www.pillconnect.com/.

[27] https://www.medgadget.com/2020/02/smarttab-wireless-pill-for-targeted-drug-delivery-interview-with-ceo-robert-niichel.html.

as well the location of the cancer in real time, after which it transmits the data to an external device.

Prescription digital therapeutics (PDTs) are poised to revolutionize health care, offering robust solutions to mitigate medication errors and enhance patient safety. By leveraging technology's power, they enable a more proactive, personalized, and patient-centric approach to care, fundamentally shifting the way we prevent, manage, and treat health conditions. The Digital Therapeutic Alliance defines PDTS as "evidence-based therapeutic interventions that are driven by high-quality software programs to treat, manage, or prevent a disease or disorder."[28] Unlike wellness apps, PDTs require a prescription from a licensed health care provider. They are studied for safety and efficacy in clinical trials and are authorized by the FDA. Because PDTs are delivered through software, not pharmacotherapy, they do not cause medication-related adverse events or drug-drug interactions. While different PDTs have different risk profiles, those on the market today are associated with limited adverse events. By digitizing therapies, PDTs can provide treatment in a standardized format, ensuring that every person who uses them receives the same quality and level of care. This is especially important in light of concerns about health care equity. Research has shown that digital disease management can drive a 45 percent reduction in the three-month rate of major adverse cardiovascular events and a 50 percent reduction in the thirty-day readmission rates for patients after acute myocardial infarction.[29]

Since PDTs are primarily provided through smart devices, they can be closely related to the user's daily life and perform continuous active interventions. Owing to these characteristics, PDTs have been developed for the main objective of chronic disease management, drug abuse prevention, sleep management, and psychological and psychiatric disease management and treatment that require continuous interaction.

There are two main types of PDTs.

---

[28] Digital Therapeutics Alliance. "Digital Therapeutics Definition and Core Principles," https://dtxalliance.org/ (2019).
[29] https://www.mckinsey.com/industries/life-sciences/our-insights/the-health-benefits-and-business-potential-of-digital-therapeutics.

1. Some PDTs digitally deliver standardized versions of behavioral therapies that are already being used as part of clinician-delivered treatment and, because they are computerized, they do not require as much clinician time. Some examples include the following:

    - reSET®—Community Reinforcement Approach plus Contingency Management for substance abuse
    - Somryst®—cognitive behavioral therapy for insomnia
    - MahanaTM—an app that uses cognitive behavioral therapy to reduce irritable bowel syndrome symptom severity

2. Others use unique, custom-designed software that offers novel treatments not traditionally delivered through clinician-delivered care, because those modalities require complex algorithmic computations. Some examples include the following:

    - EndeavorRx®—a video game for ADHD that targets the areas of the brain associated with attention function
    - NightWareTM—a wearable device that uses vibration to interrupt nightmares
    - Endeavor Rx[30]

THE ENDEAVORRX VIDEO GAME
A NOVEL DIGITAL THERAPY FOR ADHD IN CHILDREN

---

[30] https://www.endeavorrx.com/about-endeavorrx/.

At the time of publication, there are currently fourteen PDTs authorized by the FDA for use across eleven diseases.

PDT	Disease/Disorder
reSET®	Substance use disorder
reSET-O®	Opioid use disorder
Somryst®	Chronic insomnia
EndeavorRx®	ADHD
Mahana™	Irritable bowel syndrome (IBS)
Regulora®	Irritable bowel syndrome (IBS)
Ieva®	Urinary and fecal incontinence
NightWare™	Posttraumatic stress disorder (PTSD)
Freespira®	Posttraumatic stress disorder (PTSD)
Luminopia™	Amblyopia
BiovitalsHF® V1	Heart failure
Bluestar®	Type I diabetes, Type II diabetes
iSage Rx™	Diabetes
Insulia®	Diabetes

Digital therapeutics can also enhance patient safety by enabling early detection and intervention in case of health deterioration. Propeller Health's digital therapeutic solution for asthma and COPD patients is a case in point. It comprises sensor-attached inhalers that track medication use and provide feedback to patients and physicians. If a patient starts using their rescue inhaler more frequently—a sign of deteriorating lung function—the system sends an alert, allowing for early intervention and potentially preventing a severe exacerbation. Digital therapeutics like Biofourmis's Biovitals platform use wearable sensors to monitor patients' vital signs and physiological data in real time. The platform uses AI algorithms to detect signs of health deterioration, alerting health care providers so that they can intervene before a critical event occurs. This proactive approach can prevent hospitalizations and enhance patient safety. Finally, digital therapeutics, such as Pear Therapeutics's reSET and reSET-O, provide a digital approach to substance use disorder and opioid use disorder treatment. These platforms offer cognitive behavioral therapy, motivation enhancement therapy, and contingency management to patients, reducing the risk of harm associated with substance misuse. As digital therapeutics fundamentally alter our approach to health care, shifting the focus from reactive to proactive management, successful integration of digital therapeutics into health care systems will require careful implementation, robust clinical validation, regulatory oversight, and user education to ensure these tools are used effectively and safely.

The important requirements for efficient PDTs are digital adequacy aspects such as the user's ability to use digital devices and cognitive level. Since PDTs are mostly provided in the form of content through digital platforms, the higher the user's ability to use the digital device, the better the understanding and concentration on the provided content, and the higher the efficacy of the developer's intention. However, these characteristics of PDTs can cause a digital health gap due to digital disparities; therefore, a design process considering patient equity is required. Additionally, to secure the therapeutic effect of PDT, patient engagement is key and can be affected by sociocultural background and demographic characteristics. The fact that PDTs are influenced by demographic or sociocultural characteristics is not sufficiently empirically proven. However, from the examples of common digital media, we can infer that users' influence on digital content varies according to external factors. A study that analyzed the factors affecting digital media user acceptance indicated that a reader's awareness, interest, and intention to use e-books are affected by the reader's age, education level, and income. It has been reported that digital disparities or e-service discrepancies may occur depending on education level or age in the EU and income, education level, residence type, and age in Canada. In addition, it has been reported that the ability to use a mobile health app is also related to age, education level, and e-health literacy. Since PDTs are a type of digital content, we can easily infer that the above factors directly affect PDT adequacy.[31]

Diagnostic errors occur in about 5 percent of adults in outpatient care settings, more than half of which have the potential to cause severe harm. Most people will suffer a diagnostic error in their lifetime. Artificial intelligence has the potential to significantly reduce diagnostic errors in health care, and its role in health care is rapidly expanding. AI technologies, such as machine learning (ML) and natural language processing (NLP), have the potential to significantly reduce diagnostic errors by augmenting human cognition and improving access to relevant patient data. Machine-learning algorithms can analyze large amounts of patient data sets to identify patterns and risk factors and predict patient outcomes, which can aid health care providers in making accurate diagnoses. Artificial intelligence can also help to address some of the communication breakdowns that contribute to diagnostic errors. Natural language processing can improve the accuracy of HER documentation and reduce the associated clinician burden, making it easier for providers to access relevant patient information and communicate more effectively with each other.

In health care, AI can be used to analyze medical images, laboratory results, genomic data, and EHRs to identify potential diagnoses and flag patients who may be at risk for diagnostic errors. One of the primary benefits of AI in health care is its ability to process large amounts of data quickly and accurately. This can be particularly valuable in diagnosing rare or complex conditions. Machine-learning algorithms can analyze patient data to identify subtle patterns that may not be apparent to human providers. This can lead to earlier and more accurate diagnoses, which can reduce diagnostic errors and improve patient outcomes. Some examples are the following:

1. AI diagnoses occlusive myocardial infarction better than physicians with EKGs in over 7,000 consecutive patients.[32]

---

[31] https://medicalfuturist.com/drugs-vs-digital-therapeutics-a-symbiotic-rivalry/.
[32] https://www.nature.com/articles/s41591-023-02396-3.

2. AI assists cancer diagnosis and prognosis.[33]
3. Deep learning algorithms have been found to have equivalent sensitivity and specificity to health care professionals in disease diagnosis using images.[34]
4. AI can help radiologists detect abnormalities in medical images that may be missed by the human eye, such as early-stage breast cancer.[35]

AI and machine-learning algorithms can significantly improve diagnostic accuracy, reducing the risk of misdiagnoses and delayed treatment. These tools can also aid in predicting patient health trajectories, identifying high-risk patients, and implementing timely interventions, further minimizing potential harm.

Telemedicine and remote patient monitoring tools contribute to patient safety by allowing for continuous monitoring and immediate intervention in case of any abnormalities. They also enable patients to receive care from the comfort of their homes, reducing the risks associated with hospital-acquired infections. Telemedicine ensures that patients receive timely care, especially in emergencies, reducing harm from delayed treatment. One of the best examples of the safety benefit of digital health is in critical care medicine, in which teleICU programs have been associated with reduced mortality, length of intensive care unit (ICU) and hospital stay, and improved safety. In one study, a tele-ICU program implemented in 450 ICU beds across five states was associated with significant reductions in ICU-related malpractice claims from seventy claims annually to thirty claims annually and incurred

---

[33] https://www.nature.com/articles/s41591-023-02332-5.
[34] https://www.thelancet.com/journals/landig/article/PIIS2589-7500(19)30123-2/fulltext#seccestitle130.
[35] Lehman, C. D., Wellman, R. D., Buist, D. S., et al. "Diagnostic Accuracy of Digital Screening Mammography with and without Computer-Aided Detection." *JAMA Intern Med.* 15;175(11):1828–1837. doi:10.1001/jamainternmed.2015.5231.

costs from $6 million annually to $0.5 million annually within a year of program implementation.[36]

Unsafe surgical care procedures cause complications in up to 25 percent of patients. Almost 7 million surgical patients suffer significant complications annually, 1 million of whom die during or immediately following surgery. Although surgeons often use checklists before a procedure to avoid potential mistakes, a study found that postoperative complications occur in as many as 15.5 percent of surgeries, leading to more than $19,000 in increased hospital costs per surgery. At the University of Florida, researchers have created an AI system called MySurgeryRisk that predicts which patients have a higher risk of postsurgery complications and may need more care during or after an operation. A study of sixty-seven surgeons[37] who used the algorithm found that the surgeons' initial predictions were more likely to underestimate the risk of certain complications, such as blood clot formation, and overestimate the risk of others, such as severe sepsis. After using the algorithm, the accuracy of surgeons' repeated risk assessment improved.

Smart pills have revolutionized the diagnosis of gastrointestinal disorders and could replace conventional diagnostic techniques such as endoscopy. Traditionally, an endoscopy probe is inserted into a patient's esophagus, and subsequently the upper and lower gastrointestinal tract, for diagnostic purposes. There is a risk of perforation or tearing of the esophageal lining, and the patient faces discomfort during and after the procedure. Minnesota-based Medtronic offers an FDA-cleared smart pill called PillCam COLON,[38] which provides clear visualization of the colon. It is an alternative for patients who refuse invasive colon exams, have bleeding or sedation risks or inflammatory bowel disease, or have had a previous incomplete colonoscopy.

---

[36] Lilly, C. M., Zubrow, M. T., Kempner, K. M., et al. "Critical Care Telemedicine: Evolution and State of the Art." *Crit Care Med.* 2014;42(11):2429–2436.
[37] https://jamanetwork.com/journals/jamanetworkopen/fullarticle/2792367.
[38] https://www.medtronic.com/covidien/en-us/products/capsule-endoscopy/pillcam-sb3-system.html.

Pillcam[38]

Extended reality (XR) technologies like augmented, virtual, and mixed reality (AR, VR, and MR) will play a major role in improving surgical safety and accessibility. Here are a few ways these technologies can improve surgical safety:

- preoperative planning and simulation. XR can provide an immersive, 3D view of a patient's anatomy derived from their medical imaging data, enabling surgeons to plan operations more accurately. Surgeons can rehearse complex procedures ahead of time, which can lead to fewer surprises during the actual surgery and improved patient outcomes. For example, Surgical Theater's VR platform is used for neurosurgical planning.
- intraoperative navigation. During surgery, AR can overlay digital information onto the surgeon's field of view, which can guide surgical interventions. These AR projections can include the patient's medical imaging data, effectively allowing the surgeon to "see through" tissues. This can improve the precision of surgical maneuvers, reducing the risk of harm to surrounding structures.
- surgical training. XR is revolutionizing surgical education. With VR, trainees can practice procedures in a simulated environment, which allows for learning from mistakes without any risk to patients. Furthermore, AR can provide real-time

guidance during actual surgical procedures, enhancing the learning experience.
- patient education. XR can also be used to educate patients about their surgical procedure, helping them understand what to expect. Better-informed patients are more likely to engage in preoperative and postoperative care activities, which can lead to better surgical outcomes.
- telesurgery. Using VR, a surgeon can control a robotic system to perform surgery on a patient who is not in the same physical location. This can extend the reach of expert surgeons, especially in areas with limited access to surgical care.

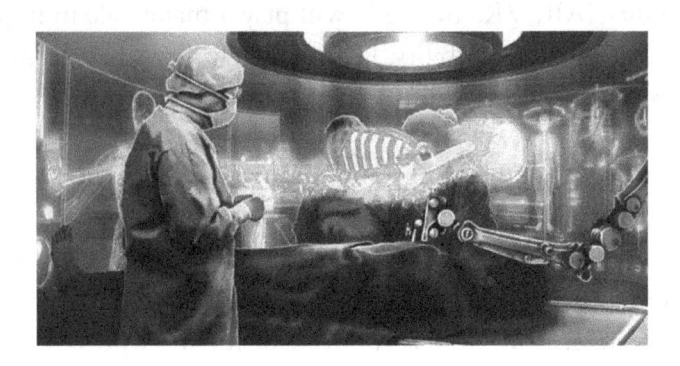

Extended Reality in Surgery[39]

However, while the potential of XR in improving surgical safety is enormous, it's crucial to address challenges, such as the accuracy and reliability of XR systems, the seamless integration of these technologies into surgical workflows, and the resolution of any potential side effects, such as cybersickness, associated with the use of XR technologies. As these technologies continue to advance and mature, they will likely play an increasingly important role in ensuring surgical safety.

Sepsis is frequently not diagnosed early enough to save a patient's life. Because these infections are often resistant to antibiotics, they can

---

[39] https://pubmed.ncbi.nlm.nih.gov/36645474/#:~:text=Purpose%3A%20Extended%20reality%20(XR),also%20in%20research%20and%20development.

rapidly lead to deteriorating clinical conditions, affecting an estimated 31 million people worldwide and causing over 5 million deaths per year. Digital technology can play a significant role in reducing the incidence of sepsis by aiding in early detection, improving management, and enhancing the overall understanding of the condition. Electronic health records (EHRs) combined with Clinical Decision Support Systems (CDSS) can be used to identify early signs of sepsis in patients. For instance, Epic's EHR system includes a sepsis screening tool that uses laboratory results and vital sign data to alert health care providers to potential cases of sepsis.

AI and Machine-Learning Algorithms

AI and machine learning can be used to analyze large amounts of patient data and identify patterns that might suggest sepsis. Cerner's St. John Sepsis Agent is an example of a machine-learning-based system that helps detect sepsis. Wearable devices can monitor patients' vital signs and other relevant data continuously, which can help detect sepsis early. For instance, the Philips Guardian System uses wearable biosensors to continuously monitor patients and alert health care providers to signs of clinical deterioration that could indicate sepsis. Telemedicine platforms can be used to monitor patients remotely, enabling the timely detection and management of sepsis. Advanced ICU Care, a tele-ICU provider, offers remote patient monitoring that has helped hospitals detect sepsis early and initiate appropriate treatment.

A key problem with sepsis is that it cannot be detected accurately and quickly enough to initiate the right course of treatment. In patients who have been infected by an unknown pathogen and progress to overt sepsis, every additional hour that an effective antibiotic cannot be administered significantly increases the mortality rate, so time is of utmost essence. A multidisciplinary team at Harvard's Wyss Institute for Biologically Inspired Engineering and the University of Bath, UK, has also developed the eRapid technology, a low-cost electrochemical diagnostic sensor platform for the detection of sepsis at the point of care within three to seven minutes.[40]

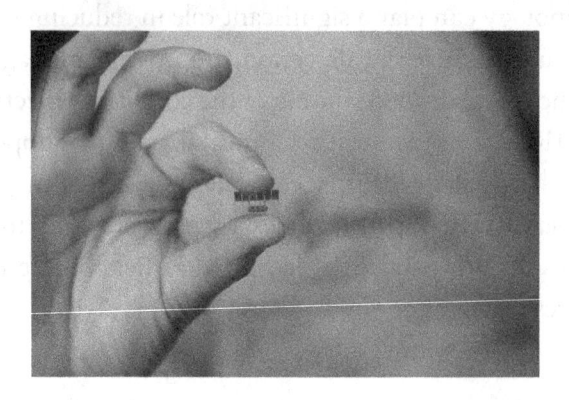

eRapid[41]

It's important to note that while these technologies hold promise, sepsis is a complex condition that requires comprehensive care. Technology should be seen as a tool to assist clinicians, not as a replacement for clinical judgment. Furthermore, the successful implementation of these technologies requires adequate staff training and robust data security measures.

Unsafe injection practices (for medication administration and blood draws) in health care settings can transmit infections, including HIV and hepatitis B and C, and pose direct danger to patients and health care workers; they account for a burden of harm estimated at 9.2 million years of life lost to disability and death worldwide (known as disability adjusted life years or DALYs). Augmented reality (AR) can assist health

---

[40] https://www.technologynetworks.com/diagnostics/news/sensor-enables-fast-accurate-and-cheap-detection-of-multiple-sepsis-biomarkers-345607.
[41] https://wyss.harvard.edu/technology/erapid-multiplexed-electrochemical-sensors-for-fast-accurate-portable-diagnostics/.

care providers in finding the best injection site. For instance, AccuVein[42] uses AR to visualize a patient's veins, aiding in successful venipuncture and reducing the risk of multiple needle insertion attempts.

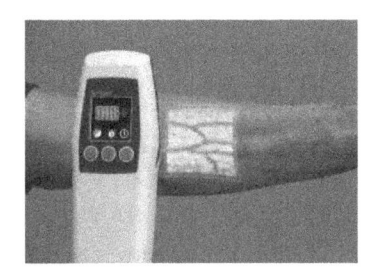

Accuvein[42]

As the call for noninvasive point-of-care testing increases, smart pills will become mainstream devices. The term "smart pills" refers to miniature electronic devices that are shaped and designed in the mold of pharmaceutical capsules but perform highly advanced functions, such as sensing, imaging, and drug delivery. They may include biosensors or image, pH or chemical sensors. Proteus Digital Health offers an FDA-approved microchip, an ingestible pill that tracks medication-taking behavior and how the body is responding to medicine. The sensor monitors blood flow, body temperature, and other vital signs for people with heart problems, schizophrenia, or Alzheimer's disease. A similar pill from HQ Inc. called the CorTemp Ingestible Core Body Temperature Sensor transmits real-time body temperature. Medimetrics has developed a pill called IntelliCap with drug reservoir, pH, and temperature sensors that release drugs to a defined region of the gastrointestinal tract. The miniaturization of electronic components has been crucial to smart pill design. As cloud computing and wireless communication platforms are integrated into the health care system, the

---

[42] https://www.accuvein.com/inf-landing-page/?utm_source=google&utm_medium=cpc&utm_campaign=vein-campaign&utm_content=&utm_term=accuvein%20vein%20finder&gclid=CjwKCAjw5MOlBhBTEiwAAJ8e1nH-clXtyOIAMUZ1Jz-p0CI2HD_sFDMStGbWcbSzCZUo-B91r3KaWRoCNqIQAvD_BwE.

use of smart pills for monitoring vital signs and medication compliance is likely to increase. In the long term, smart pills are expected to be an integral component of remote patient monitoring and telemedicine.

A digital twin is a virtual representation of a physical entity. In health care, a digital twin of a patient can integrate diverse data sources, including electronic health records, genetic data, lifestyle information, and data from wearable devices, to create a comprehensive and dynamic representation of the patient's health. It can also guide personalized treatment strategies, reducing trial-and-error approaches and potentially harmful side effects. "Digital biopsies" and "digital diagnostics" enable both depth and breadth of information for a particular patient facilitating precision medicine and fine-tuning patient care to molecular and genomic levels minimizing the need for invasive procedures and reducing potential harm.

Rapid advancement in mobile digital health technologies has given consumers greater control over their care and the ability to engage more deeply with providers. Digital health tools can enhance patient engagement, a critical aspect of patient safety. Apps and wearables encourage patients to take a proactive role in managing their health, providing them with vital information and alerting them when they need medical attention. Improved patient engagement can lead to better adherence to treatment plans and early detection of potential health issues. Here are some key considerations to improve patient engagement when introducing digital health technologies.

- ease of use. A digital health platform should be user-friendly. If the interface is difficult to navigate or understand, patients might feel overwhelmed and disengage. Simplifying the user interface and ensuring compatibility with various devices can significantly increase patient engagement.
- accessibility. The platform should be accessible to all patients, regardless of their location, age, or tech-savviness. Consider factors like language options, compatibility with assistive technologies, and ease of use on different devices (desktop, mobile, tablet). Additionally, ensure the platform is compatible

with various internet speeds to cater to patients in areas with slower internet connections.
- education and training. Educate patients about the benefits and functionalities of the platform. This might involve creating educational materials or providing training sessions. Additionally, continuous support should be available to help patients troubleshoot any issues that arise.
- personalization. Offering personalized features can significantly enhance patient engagement. This might involve tailoring health information to the patient's specific condition, offering personalized health recommendations, or allowing patients to customize the platform's settings to their preferences.
- communication. Digital health platforms should facilitate seamless communication between patients and health care providers. This could involve enabling secure messaging, video consultations, or feedback mechanisms. Quick responses from health care providers can foster trust and increase patient engagement.
- data privacy and security. Patients are more likely to engage with the platform if they trust it with their health information. Therefore, ensure robust data privacy and security measures are in place, and communicate these measures clearly to the patients.
- integration with existing systems. The digital health platform should be able to integrate with existing health systems, like EHRs, to offer a seamless health care experience. This can make the platform more convenient and useful for patients, thereby enhancing engagement.
- patient involvement. Involve patients in the design and development process. Their feedback can offer valuable insights into what features they find useful, what concerns they have, and how the platform can be improved to better meet their needs.

From a disruption perspective, however, a growing evidence base also highlights the risks attached to new digital technologies. New technologies parachuted into organizations can increase cognitive burden for staff, exacerbating the risk of error. Oversights in user-centered design and unanticipated malfunctions can result in unintentional error that is both costly and damaging. In today's tech-driven society, providers and health care organizations simply cannot serve patients well when there are significant gaps in employees' technology experience. It's almost impossible to fully engage the health care workforce in delivering better patient outcomes when technology is a hinderance rather than a help. Here are a few examples:

- data overload. Digital health technologies can generate a vast amount of data, which can overwhelm physicians and other health care professionals. If not properly managed, this data overload can lead to missed critical information or delayed decision-making, which can potentially compromise patient safety.
- workflow disruption. Implementing new digital health technologies can disrupt established clinical workflows, leading to confusion or errors. For instance, a poorly designed EHR system can increase the complexity of tasks, leading to longer work hours for physicians and increasing the risk of burnout, which can indirectly impact patient safety.
- cybersecurity threats. Digital health technologies are vulnerable to cybersecurity threats, such as hacking or ransomware attacks. If a cyberattack results in unauthorized access to a patient's health information or disrupts a health care provider's ability to access crucial health data, it can directly jeopardize patient safety.
- software errors and malfunctions. Digital health technologies, like any software, are not immune to glitches, malfunctions, or errors. For example, a malfunction in a computerized physician order entry (CPOE) system could lead to incorrect medication orders, potentially causing harm to patients.

- training and usability issues. The use of digital health technologies often requires specific skills and training. Lack of adequate training or usability issues can lead to user errors or nonoptimal use of the technologies, potentially compromising patient safety.
- overreliance on technology. There's a risk that health professionals might rely too much on technology at the expense of their clinical judgment. For instance, if a clinician overly relies on a clinical decision support system, they might miss signs of a patient's deteriorating condition if the system fails to flag it.
- interoperability challenges. Digital health technologies often need to integrate with existing health systems and share data effectively. However, interoperability challenges can lead to fragmented or incomplete health records, potentially impacting the quality of care and patient safety.

While these challenges are real, they can be mitigated with appropriate strategies, such as comprehensive training, robust cybersecurity measures, thorough software testing, and user-centered design. Stakeholders must be aware of these potential issues and proactively address them to ensure the safe and effective use of digital health technologies.

Despite the beneficial associations between digital health and patient safety, several safety concerns need to be addressed. One is the quality of the software applications being produced. Many app developers do not have medical training and often do not involve medical experts in the design process. Furthermore, many of these applications do not undergo rigorous evaluation before deployment for general use, and some studies suggest that some unsafe apps are on the market. For example, in one systematic assessment of forty-six smartphone apps for calculating insulin dose based on planned carbohydrate intake, 67 percent of these apps were associated with inappropriate output dose recommendations that put users at risk of both catastrophic overdose and more subtle harms resulting from suboptimal glucose control.[43]

Yes, while digital technology offers significant potential to improve patient safety, it also presents new risks related to data security, privacy, and integrity. The following are a few key concerns:

- data breaches. Health data is sensitive and highly valuable, making it a prime target for cybercriminals. Data breaches can lead to unauthorized access to patients' health information, potentially resulting in identity theft, fraud, or harm to the patient if their data is manipulated.
- data privacy. In the era of digital health records and telemedicine, maintaining the privacy of health information is challenging. Unauthorized access or leakage of sensitive health information can lead to stigmatization or discrimination.
- data integrity. The accuracy and consistency of data over its entire life cycle are crucial in health care. Errors in data entry, transmission, or storage can lead to misinformation, potentially causing harm to patients.
- reliability and availability of systems. If a digital system fails, becomes unavailable, or provides inaccurate information, it could lead to delayed or incorrect treatment. Dependence on technology for crucial health services means that system downtime or malfunctions can directly impact patient safety.
- inadequate training and user errors. Digital health technologies often require specific skills to operate effectively. Inadequate training can lead to user errors, misinterpretation of data, or nonoptimal use of the technologies, potentially impacting patient safety.
- dependence on technology: Health professionals face the danger of leaning excessively on technological tools, potentially sidelining their clinical expertise. For instance, should a clinician

---

[43] Huckvale, K., Adomaviciute, S., Prieto, J. T., Leow, M. K., Car, J. "Smartphone Apps for Calculating Insulin Dose: A Systematic Assessment." *BMC Med.* 2015;13: 106.

become too dependent on a clinical decision support system, they could overlook indicators of a patient's worsening state if the system doesn't highlight them.

To mitigate these risks, health care innovators and organizations must employ robust data security measures, enforce strict privacy policies, ensure system reliability, and provide proper training to staff. Additionally, the use of standards and interoperability protocols can help prevent data corruption or loss during transmission between different systems. Regulation also plays a critical role in ensuring that digital health technologies are used in a way that maximizes patient safety while minimizing risks.

We recommend a comprehensive framework for organizations looking to improve patient safety outcomes when using digital health technology that includes the following:

- health information governance. Organizations must establish a health information oversight mechanism that includes leadership and relevant stakeholders. In addition, organizations need to ensure that their health information plan is coordinated with the organization's patient safety and risk management plan.
- safety risk identification. Organizations need to identify areas that health information technology might aid in improving patient safety namely, medication safety, guideline adherence, and so forth.
- stakeholder involvement. Stakeholders need to be involved in all phases of health information projects from planning and implementation until continuous improvement. The most important stakeholder must be the system end user and process owner.
- informed decision. Organizations need to review the cost effectiveness of suggested technologies, which include conducting an evidence-based decision and an evaluation of the current information technology infrastructure including software and hardware.

- sufficient training. Organizations need to ensure that all relevant line staff receive sufficient training on the use of the proposed health information technology.
- gradual implementation. Rolling out the technology in a gradual stepped approach is crucial to avoid disruption of current processes and systems.
- continuous evaluation and monitoring of patient safety outcomes. Organizations need to measure patient safety outcomes on a continuous basis, especially during the initial implementation, to ensure that the new technology achieves its intended outcome.
- technology optimization. Organizations need to modify and fine-tune the implemented technology based on user feedback and patient safety outcomes.
- regular technology updates. Organizations must ensure that health information technologies are continuously updated to comply with recent best clinical practices, regulatory standards, and technical stability.

As we conclude this chapter on the journey to zero harm through digital health, we find ourselves standing at the precipice of a health care revolution. The goal of zero harm, once an idealistic vision, now seems a tangible reality thanks to the leaps and bounds made by digital health technology. Throughout this chapter, we have seen how innovative digital tools and practices can reshape the way we approach patient safety. We've explored how artificial intelligence, telemedicine, electronic health records, and other digital tools can significantly reduce the risk of harm, ensuring that each patient receives the right care at the right time in a safe manner.

Yet despite the enormous potential of digital technology, we are reminded that it is not a cure-all. We must approach this digital revolution with thoughtfulness and caution. It's vital to ensure that the implementation of these technologies does not inadvertently introduce new types of harm or exacerbate health care disparities. Moreover, the integration of digital technology into health care must be guided by the central tenet of medicine: "Primum non nocere." ("First, do no harm.") Technology should enhance, not replace, human expertise and judgment. A patient's health and safety should always take precedence over technological advancement.

Moving forward, the path to zero harm will need a strong commitment from all stakeholders—innovators, health care providers, policymakers, and patients. We need a sustained focus on developing and implementing digital health solutions that are evidence based, user centered, and ethically designed. The journey to zero harm is not easy, but we have seen that it is possible. As we continue on this path, let us harness the power of digital health technology not just to reimagine health care but to create a system where harm is the exception, not the rule. The quest for zero harm isn't just a noble pursuit; it's an essential stride toward perfect health care.

ZERO WAIT

AS WE DELVE into the next leg of our journey, we pivot toward a paradigm shift that mirrors the Copernican revolution. In the same way that Copernicus disrupted our understanding of the universe by positioning the sun, not Earth, at the center, digital health is driving a shift in health care—from a system that requires patients to adapt to it to one that revolves around the needs and convenience of patients. One of the significant components of this shift is the aspiration toward zero wait time.

Waiting is an all-too-familiar aspect of health care—waiting for appointments, waiting for test results, waiting for treatments. These delays not only inconvenience patients but can also have serious implications for their health outcomes. As health care embraces the patient-centered approach, the concept of zero wait time emerges as a key goal, symbolizing prompt and efficient care. Digital health technology offers the potential to dramatically reduce, if not eliminate, these waiting times. From online scheduling and telemedicine consultations to AI-powered diagnostics and real-time monitoring, digital tools can streamline processes, optimize resources, and accelerate decision-making.

In this chapter, we will delve into the myriad ways in which digital technology can enable zero wait time in health care. We will explore successful examples, understand potential obstacles, and envisage future innovations. We will examine how a shift toward patient-centric care, facilitated by digital technology, can transform not only the patient experience but also the overall efficiency and effectiveness of health care delivery. In our pursuit of zero wait, we are not just aiming for quicker care. We are striving for a fundamental shift in health care delivery, one where the system revolves around the patient. The journey toward zero wait time is a journey toward a truly patient-centered health care system. Let's explore this exciting transformation together.

Here's an easy way to think about it: Imagine if instead of having to go to the doctor's office when you're sick, the doctor's office comes to you, wherever you are. It could be through a video call on your phone (telemedicine), a health monitoring device you wear (like a smartwatch), or even an app on your phone that helps you manage your health. In a recent study to evaluate the relationship between clinic and ambulatory blood pressure and mortality,[44] ambulatory blood pressure, particularly nighttime blood pressure, was more informative about the risk of all-cause death and cardiovascular death than clinic blood pressure—six times more predictive! Therefore, the traditional approach of measuring blood pressure in health care settings is not a good predictor of outcomes.

Blood pressure monitoring is an essential part of a patient's examination. The history of blood pressure monitoring originates in the sixteenth century from Sir Stephen Hales's experiments involving directly inserting a tube in an artery. Since then, the practice has been (thankfully) improved not to involve invasive maneuvers. The practice with which we are more accustomed hails from the twentieth century. This has traditionally involved a combination of an inflatable arm cuff, a stethoscope, and a mercury-based scale, and historically the purview of medical practitioners performed in traditional care delivery systems.

With the advent of digital health, the means to measure blood pressure are evolving and are enabling patients to record their readings and share them with their doctors. Companies like iHealth, Withings, and Viatom have even added extra features, such as heart rate monitoring and the integration of BP and ECG monitors, into single devices. These can pair with a companion smartphone app to store the collected data. This allows patients to further analyze or share the results, thereby enabling them to better manage their condition at home. Omron developed the first-ever blood pressure smartwatch. Unlike other BP monitors, this wearable can take BP measurements from the wrist with

---

[44] https://www.thelancet.com/journals/lancet/article/PIIS0140-6736(23)00733-X/fulltext.

cuffs integrated in the strap, and it even has FDA-clearance for blood pressure readings.

Omron Wearable Blood Pressure Monitor[45]

Newer approaches are more promising, especially with devices using photoplethysmography (PPG). PPG is a noninvasive optical technique that provides measurements based on changes in light intensity as a result of blood flow. Adopting PPG sensors results in sleeker devices that are much more practical. They can further be more convenient as they can enable continuous, real-time BP readings as opposed to one-off measurements at the doctor's office. For example, the Akita smart bracelet is lightweight and designed to continuously monitor blood pressure throughout the day. Its readings have even been shown to be comparable to traditional cuff-based BP monitors. Other PPG-based devices like the BioBeat smart patch aim to monitor BP without visibly doing so. The sensor is applied through a skin patch on the body for reliable twenty-four-hour monitoring. Recently the FDA cleared Casana's smart toilet seat.[46] Using sensors embedded in the toilet seat, the device is able to measure these vital signs and send the

---

[45] https://omronhealthcare.com/products/heartguide-wearable-blood-pressure-monitor-bp8000m/.

[46] https://www.mobihealthnews.com/news/casana-scores-fda-clearance-health-monitoring-toilet-seat.

data automatically to the Casana Cloud. From there, a designated health care provider is able to view the data generated from the three sensors: a ballistocardiogram (which measures the mechanical activity of the heart), an electrocardiogram (which measures the electrical activity of the heart), and a photoplethysmogram (which detects blood volume changes). This evolution is an excellent showcase of how digital technology continues to progress to empower patient to be the point of care thereby eliminating waiting times.

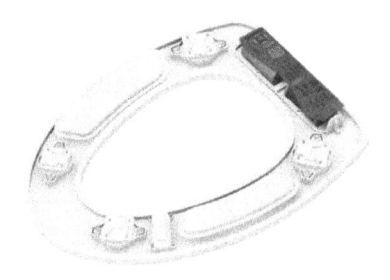

Casana Heart Seat[47]

Long wait times are a prevalent issue within health care systems globally, contributing to patient dissatisfaction and potentially impacting health outcomes. A Commonwealth Fund survey of eleven countries in 2017[48] found that adults in the United States faced the longest wait times for specialist appointments. In the survey, 30 percent of US adults reported waiting six days or more for a specialist appointment, while the median wait time was five days across the other ten countries. In Canada, wait times for medical procedures have been a significant concern. A

---

[47] https://casanacare.com/the-heart-seat/.
[48] The Commonwealth Fund. (2017). "Mirror, Mirror 2017: International Comparison Reflects Flaws and Opportunities for Better US Health Care." Retrieved from. https://www.commonwealthfund.org/publications/fund-reports/2017/jul/mirror-mirror-2017-international-comparison-reflects-flaws-and.

report by the Fraser Institute in 2019[49] indicated that the median wait time between referral from a general practitioner to treatment was 20.9 weeks, significantly longer than the three weeks experienced in 1993. In the UK, the National Health Service (NHS) has a standard target that no patient should wait longer than eighteen weeks from referral to treatment. However, by November 2019, around 4.45 million people were waiting for routine surgery, the highest ever level, according to NHS England data.[50] Prolonged wait times can lead to delayed diagnosis and treatment, potentially worsening health outcomes. For instance, a study published in the *Journal of Health Services Research* in 2017 found that prolonged wait times for colorectal cancer surgery were associated with higher mortality rates.[51] Long wait times also contribute to patient dissatisfaction and stress. A study in the *Journal of Public Health* in 2018 found that longer wait times negatively impacted patients' perception of care and trust in health care professionals.[52]

Generative AI, which uses advanced machine-learning algorithms to generate outputs like text, images, voice, or even virtual realities, has considerable potential to revolutionize health care delivery and possibly eliminate wait times. These virtual assistants can be available twenty-four/seven, offering advice, answering health-related questions, or even helping with symptom checking. Leading UK-health care business Clinova has launched Healthwords,[53] one of the world's first

---

[49] The Fraser Institute. (2019). "Waiting Your Turn: Wait Times for Health Care in Canada." Retrieved from https://www.fraserinstitute.org/studies/waiting-your-turn-wait-times-for-health-care-in-canada-2019.

[50] NHS England. (2019). NHS Waiting Times for Elective and Cancer Treatment. Retrieved from https://www.england.nhs.uk/statistics/statistical-work-areas/rtt-waiting-times/.

[51] Anantha, R. V., Inglis, K., Mastrocostas, K., Amin, M., Power, B., Driman, D., ... & Parry, N. (2017). Wait times for resection of colorectal cancer and its impact on survival. Journal of Health Services Research, 52(3), 1254–1265.

[52] Blendon, R. J., Benson, J. M., Hero, J. O., & Campbell, A. L. (2018). The Public and the Opioid-Abuse Epidemic. New England Journal of Medicine, 378(5), 407–411.

[53] https://www.healthtechdigital.com/launch-of-new-generative-ai-health-platform-will-revolutionise-self-care-and-free-up-much-needed-gp-appointments/.

conversational AI tools solely focused on providing health care advice and self-care products in the UK. The market-leading tool is set to transform the self-care industry by using a template that's similar to ChatGPT. Healthwords is an end-to-end solution for self-care, providing users with twenty-four/seven access to fast personalized health care advice based on their individual needs. When users input their question or symptom into the conversational search function, the generative AI technology will provide medically verified answers or advice and then recommend self-care products if directed to do so. Users will also have the option to read more about their condition in full-length verified medical articles or chat online with a human pharmacist in real time, should they want a second opinion. The user can then choose to purchase self-care products and arrange for them to be delivered to their homes, all through the single platform.

Healthwords is especially relevant for those who want nonurgent health care advice but don't have the time or ability to visit the pharmacist during standard working hours. While it is not designed as a replacement for visiting a medical professional, it educates users in self-care, removing the stigma or apathy associated with seeking in-person advice about certain personal symptoms. NHS England has previously reported there are 18 million primary care appointments and 2.1 million visits to A&E every year for conditions that could be dealt with at home, costing £850 million. By empowering patients across the UK with verified information that would allow them to manage self-treatable conditions instead of going to a general practitioner (GP), millions of unnecessary NHS appointments could be released. Healthwords aims to effect this change and improve efficiency in the British health care system by relieving pressure on heavily burdened GPs and freeing up appointments for those who need them most. Healthwords is soon to have the capability to provide prescription medication for common conditions, such as earache and sore throat, following the UK's government's recent announcement for patients to receive such prescriptions without a GP appointment. This facility will further support users to manage their own health, improving and modernizing access to care, another example of how digital technology can achieve zero cost and zero wait health care.

Ambient intelligence (AmI) refers to electronic environments that are sensitive and responsive to the presence of people. It integrates various elements of AI, IoT, ubiquitous computing, and contextual awareness to provide seamless, personalized, and interactive services to individuals. Amazon Go[54] uses "just walk-out technology"—sensors and cameras that track the items that each customer picks up (and puts down again). Once they are done shopping, they simply walk out of the store and their receipt will be emailed to them. There is no need to go through a checkout line or scan items as they leave, and the bill is automatically charged to their Amazon account. This checkout-free solution has the potential to revolutionize shopping experiences and has certainly caused a stir among retail employees and those who are worried about the impact this could have on jobs. Amazon Go technology succeeds in removing the last ounce of friction in the physical buying process: the checkout system! No one wants to stand in line for ten minutes, load, unload, and load their trolley or basket—time is precious—meaning Amazon Go meets every last request of the time-poor modern-day consumer. Similarly ambient intelligence can revolutionize health care in various ways, enabling instant access to services and improving the efficiency of care.

Overall, health care can learn a lot from Amazon Go in terms of how to improve the patient experience and make health care delivery more efficient. By adopting some of the same technologies and strategies that Amazon Go uses, health care can create a more seamless and personalized health care experience for patients. What's exciting about this technology is its ability to clarify the entire technology components and harmoniously blend the environment around the user—a true Copernican shift—without directly demanding the users' attention. Ambient intelligence in health care mainly involves making regular hospital and home zones "intelligent" by using contactless sensors and

---

[54] https://www.adcocksolutions.com/post/is-amazon-go-store-technology-the-end-of-supermarket-checkouts.

machine-learning algorithms to create physical spaces that are sensitive to human presence. As stated earlier, these "spaces" can communicate with humans on sensing their presence and collect their health-related data for diagnostic purposes.

Long waiting time in hospitals has always been one of the more problematic aspects of health care for patients. Ambient intelligence tools can enable hospitals to conduct preliminary tests on patients autonomously. For instance, it is easy to picture the following scenario:

An ambient intelligence sensor monitors the health condition of a waiting patient by dynamically monitoring their vitals. After collecting and closely assessing the details related to their body temperature, body fat, heart rate, pulse, cholesterol level, and BMI index, a diagnosis report can be prepared autonomously. In the report, any information regarding a potential disease is specified clearly. What's more, the AI-based tools involved in the network of ambient intelligence in health care also study the vitals before enlisting several diet and lifestyle recommendations in the report. These recommendations will contain prescribed medicines that need to be taken as well as any foods or habits that will have to be adopted or avoided by the individual to improve their health. Apart from creating a diagnostics report after evaluating waiting patients, ambient microphones in a physician's hospital room can also create a medical report based on what the doctor tells their patient during and after performing a checkup. With assistance from Natural Language Processing, such ambient microphones can digitally determine the gist of the physician's words to create the report as per the standardized medical format.

With cameras, sensors, and algorithms, it is possible to accurately and automatically track the movement and activity patterns of patients at home as well, easing the mental burden of patients, health care professionals, and relatives. Let's consider an example involving a senior patient named Maria. Maria, who is seventy-five years old, lives alone and has been recently diagnosed with type 2 diabetes and hypertension. Her children are concerned about her health and well-being, especially as Maria values her independence and wants to continue living alone.

An ambient intelligence (AmI) system is installed in Maria's home to help manage her health and ensure her safety. Here's how it works:

- health monitoring. The AmI system includes sensors and wearable devices that continuously monitor Maria's vital signs, including her blood glucose levels and blood pressure. These readings are automatically recorded and transmitted to her health care provider in real time. If there's a concerning change in her vitals, an alert is sent to her health care provider and her designated emergency contact.
- medication reminders. Maria sometimes forgets to take her medications on time. The AmI system gives her audible and visual reminders to take her medicines, improving her medication adherence.
- fall detection. The AmI system includes sensors that can detect unusual movements, such as a sudden fall. If a fall is detected, the system automatically contacts emergency services and alerts Maria's children.
- dietary management. Maria often struggles with managing her diabetes-friendly diet. The smart refrigerator in her AmI system monitors her food intake and provides suggestions for healthier food choices. It also alerts her when she's running low on a particular healthy food item.
- exercise encouragement. The AmI system reminds Maria about her daily exercise routines, helping her maintain an active lifestyle. It tracks her activities and provides feedback on her progress, keeping her motivated.
- mental health support. Maria sometimes feels lonely. Her AmI system includes an AI-powered virtual companion that she can talk to. This companion can engage her in conversations, play her favorite music, and remind her of upcoming social events in her community, helping to maintain her mental health.

With this AmI system in place, Maria is able to live independently while managing her health conditions more effectively. Her children and health care providers can have peace of mind knowing that Maria is safe, her health is being continuously monitored, and she's getting support in adhering to her treatment plan. Over time, the improved medication adherence, continuous health monitoring, and lifestyle changes contribute to better health outcomes for Maria. All of this without having to wait a single minute!

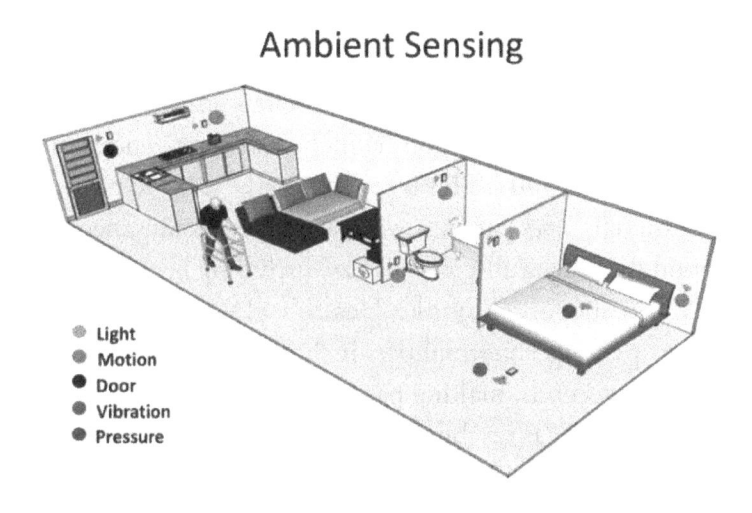

Ambient Sensing

- Light
- Motion
- Door
- Vibration
- Pressure

Ambient Sensing[55]

Another key trend that eliminates wait times is the prosumerization of health care. Prosumers are technology enabled producer of their own care—not patients and not consumers! For the first time in the history of humankind, patients now have unprecedented access to medical knowledge and the tools to not only participate in but also direct their own care. Like other industries, this disruption has the potential to shrink the role and relevance of today's health care providers and simultaneously help create better, faster, and cheaper service.

---

[55] https://www.researchgate.net/publication/224809210_A_Review_of_Wearable_Sensors_and_Systems_with_Application_in_Rehabilitation/figures?lo=1.

According to the WHO, cardiovascular diseases take the lives of 17.9 million people every year, which means 32 percent of all global death. Moreover, they are estimated to be the most expensive conditions to treat. Another common feature is that they are slow to show symptoms, which is why they're called the "silent epidemic." Early detection would be key to prevention, but that could only happen through constant monitoring as early signs of heart diseases are difficult to catch. That's why it has been so challenging to take up the fight—until the appearance of pocket-sized, user-friendly digital technologies. Eko Health, a leading innovator in digital health technology for heart and lung disease detection, launched its next-generation digital stethoscope, CORE 500™. This is the first stethoscope to provide health care professionals *and* patients with accurate, instantaneous patient auscultation data on a full-color display, including heart rate and ECG tracing. When supported by Eko Health's FDA-cleared AI products, the stethoscope flags abnormalities, including AFib, bradycardia, and tachycardia, in seconds, making patients the point of care.

Similarly, WIWE, a business card-sized, clinical-grade ECG monitor developed by Sanametal (Hungary), offers the layperson a simple and convenient way to stay on top of their heart health. It goes further than most other such devices on the market in that it offers more detailed analysis of their ECG including irregularities in the ventricular department and not only in the atrial activities. And it does this with 98.7 percent accuracy. This allows you to monitor for potential arrhythmias and risks of stroke and sudden cardiac arrest risk from the comfort of your home. It may give you an early warning that a consultation with your doctor is needed. There are also some extras, such as SpO2 measurements and the ability to count steps.

Anura™ is a mobile app built on affective AI. It uses the world's first patented Transdermal Optical Imaging (TOI™) technology that extracts facial blood flow information from the human face through a conventional video camera then processed by cloud engine. It measures and analyzes human affects that inform physiological and psychological states. Anura™ provides a plethora of health-related information like heart rate, stress, blood pressure, BMI, cardiovascular disease risks, then distills them to an overall health score that's meaningful to you—in just thirty seconds!

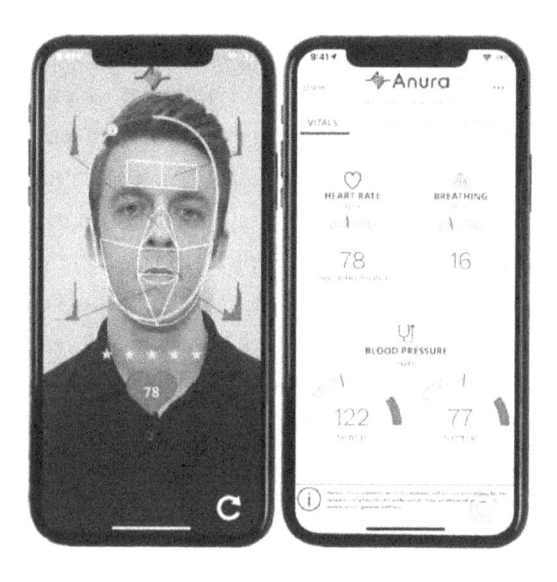

Anura[56]

There is also evidence for the potential use of the TOI technology, Anura, for truly contactless, noninvasive, and convenient assessments for diabetes management.[56] This technology has the potential to revolutionize diabetes management by predicting diabetes classifications through the use of a digital camera in a smartphone. The application of the TOI technology for monitoring diabetes would have a wide range of economic, societal, and personal benefits. A smartphone would allow people to assess and monitor their HbA1c levels anytime and anywhere, helping to keep their glycemic levels within a healthy range. In addition, if a smartphone can alert an individual at risk for diabetes or diabetes-related complications, they can seek medical attention early.

---

[56] https://www.nuralogix.ai/wp-content/uploads/2021/06/smartphone-based-identification-of-critical-levels-of-glycated-hemoglobin-a1c-using-transdermal-optical-imaging.pdf.

There is also a new kind of doctor coming to town. It will be there to help patients when they spike a fever in the middle of the night. It will reassure them when they are in pain and scared and do not know what to do. It might even be able to figure out diagnosis and treatment options. But it will not be human. The wave of chatbots is on its way to health and holds tremendous potential to empower patients to be their own point of care. A chatbot is a computer program or application that can simulate conversation with human users. Chatbots are often used in customer service applications, where they can answer questions and provide support to customers. Chatbots can also be used for other purposes, such as providing information or entertainment. Chatbots are typically powered by artificial intelligence (AI) or natural language processing (NLP) technologies. These technologies allow chatbots to understand human language and respond in a way that is both informative and engaging. Here are some of the benefits of using chatbots:

- twenty-four/seven availability. Chatbots are available twenty-four/seven, which means that users can get help or information whenever and wherever they need it.
- cost-effectiveness. Chatbots are typically more cost-effective than human customer service representatives. Usually free!
- scalability. Chatbots can be scaled to meet the needs of a growing business.
- personalization. Chatbots can be personalized to the individual user, which can improve the user experience.

Woebot[57] is a chatbot designed by researchers at Stanford University to provide mental health assistance using cognitive behavioral therapy (CBT) techniques. People who suffer from depression, anxiety disorders, or mood disorders can converse with this chatbot, which in turn helps people treat themselves by reshaping their behavior and thought patterns.

---

[57] https://topflightapps.com/ideas/chatbots-in-healthcare/.

Global health care services are becoming overstretched and harder to access, and we have to deal with unforeseen events, such as the COVID-19 pandemic, so we also need to look to AI solutions like chatbots. Babylon, a UK-based company, combines the ever-growing power of their chatbot with the best medical expertise of humans to deliver unparalleled access to health care, including personalized health assessments, treatment advice, and face-to-face appointments with a doctor twenty-four/seven. In recent years, Rwanda has been at the forefront of digital innovation in health care, largely due to its strategic partnership with Babylon Health. Babylon's "Babyl" service, launched in Rwanda in 2016, has revolutionized health care delivery, making medical consultations, prescriptions, and health advice accessible instantaneously via mobile phones. This partnership is a stellar example of how digital technology can be leveraged to provide comprehensive, accessible, and affordable health care in a low-resource setting.[58] [59] [60]

Babyl's impact in Rwanda is significant due to the country's unique health care challenges. With a widely dispersed rural population and a low doctor-to-patient ratio, access to health care has historically been a major challenge. Many Rwandans live considerable distances from the nearest health facility, making routine and emergency care difficult to obtain.

---

[58] "Babyl Rwanda." (2020). Babylon Health. https://www.babylonhealth.com/case-study/babyl-rwanda.

[59] "How digital health services are changing the face of healthcare in Rwanda." (2019). The New Times Rwanda, https://www.newtimes.co.rw/supplements/how-digital-health-services-are-changing-face-healthcare-rwanda.

[60] Rwamugema, B. (2018). "Rwanda's digital ambassadors aim to boost computer literacy." BBC News. https://www.bbc.com/news/business-44832388.

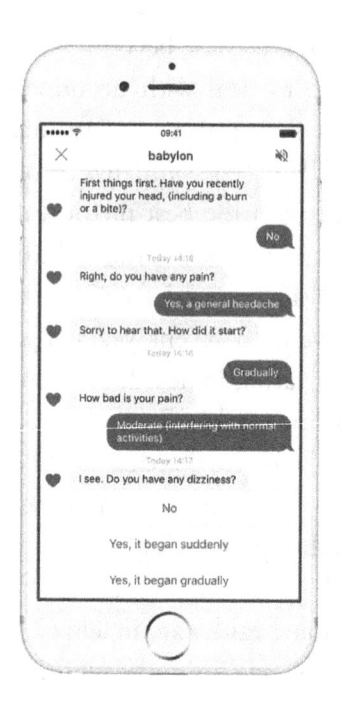

Babyl Chatbot[61]

Through its AI-powered chatbot and call center, Babylon's Babyl service has addressed these challenges by providing accessible health care directly to the people. With a mobile phone, a user can perform a symptom check using the AI chatbot or make a phone call to consult with a doctor. This ensures that individuals in even the most remote areas can receive medical advice without leaving their homes.

Moreover, the service also addresses another challenge: affordability. The cost of health care can be a significant barrier for many people in Rwanda. However, Babyl's services are covered by Rwanda's community-based health insurance system, making it financially accessible to a majority of the population at zero cost to them!

The digitization of health care services also improves efficiency. Digital records make it easier for doctors to access patient histories,

---

[61] https://www.babyl.rw/.

reducing the risk of misdiagnosis and ensuring that treatment plans are informed by the patient's overall health context. Babylon's partnership with the Rwandan government also includes training for health care professionals, contributing to capacity building and increasing the overall quality of health care.

The impact of Babylon's Babyl service in Rwanda is impressive. Since its launch, Babyl has served over 2.6 million patients and has helped to reduce the number of people who travel to health centers for care. This not only demonstrates the demand for digital health services but also underscores their potential to transform health care in low-resource settings. The success of the Babyl program in Rwanda is a powerful case study for the potential of digital health services in other parts of the world. This model could be particularly transformative in other low-resource settings with similar challenges, such as a dispersed rural population, a low doctor-to-patient ratio, and financial barriers to accessing health care.

In recent years, advancements in medical technology have resulted in the creation of innovative tools that have moved the frontier of diagnostic testing from clinical labs and hospitals directly to patients' homes. The accessibility, convenience, and immediacy of at-home medical diagnostics not only enhance patient engagement in their own health but also have the potential to revolutionize our approach to disease detection and management. One of the most common examples of at-home diagnostics is the pregnancy test, which has been used for decades, but advancements in technology have also enabled complex diagnostics to be performed at home. Today, companies like LetsGetChecked[62] and Everlywell[63] offer a variety of at-home test kits for everything from vitamin and cholesterol levels to sexually transmitted diseases and COVID-19, which have seen wide use during the pandemic.[64]

---

[62] https://www.letsgetchecked.com/diagnostics/.
[63] https://www.everlywell.com/products/.
[64] Pollock, M., et al. (2020). "Covid-19: FDA approves first home testing kit." The Lancet Digital Health. https://www.thelancet.com/journals/landig/article/PIIS2589-7500(20)30235-2/fulltext.

iCalQ[65] is a smartphone-based point-of-care diagnostic platform that aims to democratize diagnostics by making it possible for people to perform medical lab tests at home. The iCalQ platform consists of a smartphone app, a test strip reader, and a variety of test strips that can be used to measure a range of different biomarkers. The app guides users through the testing process and provides results in real time. The iCalQ platform has the potential to revolutionize the way that diagnostics are performed. By making it possible for people to perform tests at home, iCalQ can help to reduce the cost of diagnostics and improve access to care. Additionally, iCalQ can help to empower people to take control of their own health by providing them with the ability to monitor their biomarkers and identify potential health problems early on.

Healthy.io[66] transforms the smartphone camera into a medical device to deliver health care at the speed of life. The company's at-home urinalysis and digitized wound care services enable providers and health care systems to close gaps in access and care while increasing patient satisfaction. Using colorimetric analysis, computer vision, and AI, we transform the smartphone camera into a clinical-grade medical device. They currently offer four services: Minuteful Kidney, a urine albumin to creatinine ratio (ACR) test that is a powerful tool for heart and kidney health, Minuteful For Wound, which allows for better, more accurate decision-making and wound care management, Minuteful UTI to test for signs of a UTI, and Minuteful 10 for people to take routine urine tests at home.

Smartphones are undoubtedly the twenty-first century's doctor bag. They're poised to revolutionize health care the way they have transformed how we listen to music, chat with friends, read the news, pay our bills, and more. The day is not far off when these essentially smartphone-based point-of-care diagnostics would be used by most people, which would empower them to monitor and manage their own health … the prosumerization of health care. The advent of ubiquitous care at costs approaching zero is now a reality.

---

[65] https://i-calq.com/.
[66] https://healthy.io/about-us/.

We all have to hit the bathroom—that's a fact—and if you've had to head to your annual checkup, chances are the nurse has passed you that urine cup to check your health stats. For those less minded to schedule that annual exam, Withings is launching their own at-home urine tests that you can plug right into your toilet and monitor your health data.

Withings announced its launch of U-Scan,[67] a palm-sized health lab just ninety millimeters in diameter that attaches straight into your toilet's bowl. Two cartridges will be available to check various stats: a nutrition and metabolic tracker that checks pH, ketone, vitamin C levels, and more and a second one to help track women's luteinizing hormone for ovulation cycles. Each promises early detection of potential health issues while also offering actionable advice for health improvements. Results will be routed to your phone via Wi-Fi, and you can read your health insights daily on the Withings Health Mate app.

An emerging intelligent house device with potentially wide-ranging applications for health care outside of traditional medical settings is the smart mirror.[68] This fits seamlessly into the ambient home environment, blending the data collection process into the course of our daily routines. For example, one can envision collecting health data when using the mirror for shaving, brushing teeth, etc. This interface is intended to provide a convenient means for people to track their daily health with minimal effort. The five areas of medicine where the next generation of smart mirrors is likely to create new opportunities to improve the health of patients include the following:

- passive monitoring: the ability to interact with users, without directly engaging them, to monitor physiological changes and health status (emotion detection, balance measurement, skin variation, hair loss, cardiovascular risk)

---

[67] https://www.zdnet.com/home-and-office/smart-home/ces-2023-sees-the-launch-of-two-smart-toilet-sensors/.

[68] Reflecting health: smart mirrors for personalized medicine. Available from https://www.researchgate.net/publication/328810105_Reflecting_health_smart_mirrors_for_personalized_medicine [accessed July 6, 2023].

- dynamic monitoring: the ability to receive user operation/interaction as input and provide real-time response related to the input (gait analysis, cognitive performance, grip strength, voice tracker, physical therapy)
- digital biomarker detection: the automatic detection of various metrics that are useful for assessing health (heart rate, heart rate variability, blood pressure, respiratory rate, stress level, eye health)
- telemedicine: a remote interaction between the patient and physicians (vitals detection, EHR integration, personalized care, health visualization)
- health and fitness: fitness and health performance as characterized by general consumer health (not in terms of clinical care) (weight loss, body fat, activity tracking, motivation, metabolic performance, personal coaching)

Preliminary efforts show proof of concept devices that can monitor a range of physiological parameters noninvasively, detect emotional states, and infer an individual's risk for cardiometabolic diseases.

Medical Mirror[69] encourages people to track their vital signals on a daily basis. Computer vision captures an optical signal reflected off a person's face. By analyzing and detecting small deviations in such reflections attributed to pulsating blood flood, this device provides estimates of an individual's heart rate.

Lululemon Studio Mirror, Forme Studio, Fiture Mini, and Echelon Reflect[70] increase their motivation and activity throughout the day.

Wize Mirror[71] estimates cardiometabolic risk and anxiety levels from anthropometric measurements of facial features. The concept underlying Wize Mirror is that physical characteristics and facial expressions provide surrogate measures for a person's health status, all of which can be captured by standing in front of the mirror.

---

[69] https://affect.media.mit.edu/pdfs/11.Poh-etal-SIGGRAPH.pdf.
[70] https://www.cnet.com/health/fitness/best-mirror-workout/.
[71] https://www.researchgate.net/publication/301275300_Wize_Mirror_-_a_smart_multisensory_cardio-metabolic_risk_monitoring_system.

Although all of the devices highlighted above represent research prototypes, their initial demonstrations suggest encouraging results with a clear path toward addressing challenges in health care.

Digital Health (Zero Wait) for Aging Populations

Finally, a traditional approach cannot offer a continuous and longitudinal assessment of the patient and is limited to applications for which infrequent tests are sufficient; hence, it does not meet the rapidly growing health care demands of the fast-growing aging population. The application of digital technologies to assist clinical practice can address these increasing demands by offering convenient, continuous remote medical care to older patients and holds considerable promise to transform geriatric care.

In particular, wearable digital technologies are expected to provide health care professionals with continuous access to the health status of older adults and offer unique opportunities for effective remote care. Wearables can support older adults in remotely tracking chronic health conditions or ongoing treatments and monitoring for safety concerns and can do so without disrupting daily activities. For example, wearable platforms can continuously and noninvasively capture biometric and biomolecular data, which is not feasible by traditional health assessment. They can generate instantaneous alarms in cases of emergencies, such as stroke, seizure, or fall, to allow timely medical interventions. Such tools are also expected to reduce geographical inequalities by providing older adults living in rural areas with improved access to health care services. Physical wearable sensors also monitor mobility and other activity-related signals (including steps) using miniaturized motion sensors, such as accelerometers or gyroscopes. Such wearable devices can detect fall events or assess the gait disorders of patients with Parkinson's disease. For example, an ongoing, randomized trial involving two hundred older adults will evaluate the effectiveness of an Apple Watch in detecting falls. Continuous and remote monitoring of vital signs can trigger warnings of adverse events and deteriorating conditions in older adults, including the early onset of cardiovascular, neurological, and pulmonary diseases. For example, abnormal respiration rates can predict respiratory failure, elevated body temperature can indicate an infection, and abnormal ECG patterns can alert for cardiac arrest.

The use of wearable chemical sensors offers continuous noninvasive tracking of the dynamically changing chemical composition of various biofluids, such as sweat, tears, saliva, and interstitial fluid, and hence provides extremely useful molecular-level insights into the wearer's health status. Different strategies, based on electrochemical and optical measurements, have thus been explored for creating a lab-on-the-wrist platform, performing many common hospital tests of key chemical biomarkers in a noninvasive continuous manner. These include continuous monitoring of dynamically changing glucose levels in patients with diabetes, potassium ions, and the stress hormone cortisol in individuals with cardiac disease or the Parkinson's disease drug L-DOPA (also known as levodopa). Multiplexed wearable sensor arrays offer the ability to monitor a myriad of molecular markers simultaneously and hence can lead to a better diagnostic picture of the wearer's health.

There is also a growing interest in developing nonwearable sensors, based on smart home digital systems, to monitor the behavior, posture, and movement of older adults. These sensors can analyze data and alert caregivers or health care professionals of any anomalies, thereby promoting the health and safety of older adults in their homes. For example, a pending clinical trial was designed to use the Kinect camera (a device with depth-sensing capability) as a sensor for evaluating the mobility and gait of patients with Parkinson's disease in their homes for better disease management.

The graphic below shows a vision of future home-centered geriatric care powered by digital technologies and devices. A network of internet-connected sensors on the body and distributed around the home monitors the health conditions of older adults and transmits rich, dynamic data to cloud servers. The data are then analyzed by machine learning algorithms to coordinate with the remote caregiver and with autonomous wearable therapeutic devices toward optimal health care. Such care is supported by virtual visits with the physician, voice-controlled personal assistants, and social and assistive robots. AI, artificial intelligence; DIA, diastolic; SpO2, oxygen saturation; SYS, systolic.

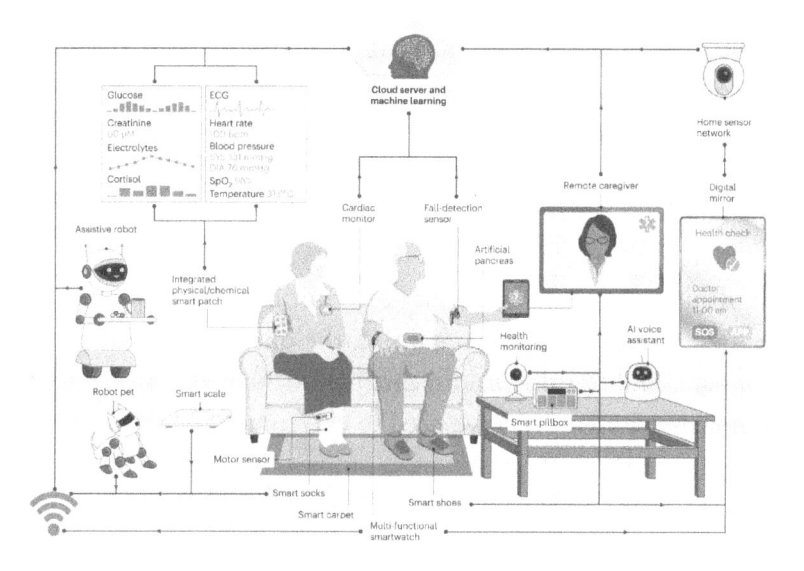

A Vision of Future Home-Centered Geriatric Care[72]

Expanding digital health services to the geriatric population will thus require simpler, user-tailored mobile devices with fewer buttons, larger text, and improved color contrast. Devices need to be user centered so that individuals with a range of other preexisting health conditions, such as impaired hearing or fragile skin, can still use and benefit from these devices. The lifetime, size, and weight of the device should also be taken into consideration. Overall, a better understanding of the technical barriers that older adults face when using digital technologies will enable designers to tailor future devices to their needs. Engaging with older adults and seeking their input on design and operation of

---

[72] https://www.nature.com/articles/s41591-023-02391-8#Fig2.

these digital devices would be the best way to understand user needs and achieve this goal.

In closing this chapter on the pursuit of zero wait times through digital health, we are left with an indelible impression of a future where health care revolves around the patient's convenience and urgency rather than the other way around. The lessons we have gathered throughout this chapter serve as a testament to the transformative potential of digital health technologies. We have seen how online scheduling systems, telemedicine, AI-assisted diagnostics, real-time monitoring, and other digital tools have drastically reduced waiting times, bringing us closer to our goal of zero wait. However, as we progress on this journey, we must be mindful of the challenges that lie ahead. Ensuring equity in access to these digital solutions, maintaining the quality of care, protecting patient data, and training health care providers to effectively use these technologies are all hurdles we need to overcome.

Yet despite these challenges, the promise of a future where health care is prompt and efficient is compelling. Imagine a health care system that is always available, that provides care when it's needed, not just when it's feasible. A system where the needs of the patient, rather than the constraints of the provider, dictate the timing of care. Digital health technology brings this vision within reach, aligning health care with the fundamental principle of patient-centeredness. The pursuit of zero wait is not just about efficiency; it symbolizes a health care system that truly serves the patient, akin to the sun-centered Copernican cosmos.

As we continue our journey to zero, the quest for zero wait time emerges as a critical milestone. A milestone that redefines the patient experience, that revolutionizes the delivery of care, and that reflects a true Copernican shift in health care. As we endeavor to make this vision a reality, let's remember that the journey, though challenging, is worth the destination—a health care system where the patient is always at the center.

ZERO STAGE

IN THIS SEGMENT of our journey to zero, we turn our attention to an emerging frontier in health care: the realm of zero stage medicine. This concept extends beyond the treatment of disease to its interception at the earliest possible stage or even its prevention. It's the embodiment of the adage "Prevention is better than cure" and echoes the principles of P4 medicine (predictive, preventive, personalized, and participatory) that increasingly guide modern health care. In a traditional health care model, intervention begins when symptoms manifest or when the disease has already progressed. In contrast, zero stage medicine aims to intervene even before the disease occurs or at its earliest inception. This paradigm shift from reaction to prevention represents a monumental change in the trajectory of a patient's health journey.

Digital health technology plays a pivotal role in enabling zero stage medicine. Advanced analytics, genomic sequencing, artificial intelligence, wearable technology, whole body scanning, and telemedicine are just a few examples of the digital tools that can help detect and manage health risks before they escalate into full-fledged diseases. In this chapter, we will explore the profound impact digital health can have in the pursuit of zero stage medicine. We will investigate successful case studies, consider the obstacles, and look ahead to future possibilities. As we examine these, we will also contemplate the philosophical shift this represents moving from a disease-centered model to one focused on prevention, wellness, and holistic well-being.

The journey toward zero stage medicine is a voyage into a new paradigm of health whereby technology empowers us to anticipate and prevent, rather than just react and treat. This proactive, preventive approach is key to the future of health care, aligning perfectly with the principles of P4 medicine. So let's venture together into this exciting evolution in our pursuit of perfect health care. The path to prevention may be technology's ultimate achievement in medicine and health!

Take the case of Parkinson's disease (PD), which is a progressive neurodegenerative movement disorder with a long latent phase and currently no disease-modifying treatments. For most patients diagnosed with Parkinson's disease, 50 percent to 70 percent of nigral dopaminergic neurons will already have degenerated by the time the hallmark motor symptoms manifest and a clinical diagnosis is made. Thus, there remains a need to identify cheap (zero cost), reliable (zero harm), easily accessible (zero wait), and sensitive biomarkers to detect early pathological changes (zero stage), with success in this field likely to be transformative in identifying suitable participants for neuroprotective therapeutics.

Recent research[73] has provided compelling evidence that accelerometry—a functionality available in most smartphones and smartwatches—is a viable digital biomarker to screen for PD. Reduced acceleration manifested years before clinical PD diagnosis. This prediagnosis reduction in acceleration was unique to PD and was not observed for any other disorder examined. Accelerometers can passively collect data continuously in real-world settings without added cost or effort, to help obtain robust estimates of a person's impairments and capabilities and detect subtle changes at the earliest possible opportunity. Such monitoring cannot be achieved through clinical assessments given the limitations of time, cost, accessibility, and sensitivity. AI coupled with accelerometers was found to predict onset of Parkinson's seven years before symptoms! A good example of how digital technology can stage zero health care!

Leroy Hood,[74] a renowned biologist and biotechnologist, is well-known for his work in the field of wellness and preventive medicine. Hood's typical disease and wellness progression integrates concepts of systems biology, big data analytics, patient-driven health care, and personalized medicine. The progression model, in line with the P4

---

[73] https://www.nature.com/articles/s41591-023-02440-2#Sec10.
[74] https://laskerfoundation.org/leroy-hood-there-is-going-to-be-a-fantastic-revolution-in-medicine/.

medicine concept, begins with a wellness phase whereby an individual is in a state of health and equilibrium. It involves regular monitoring of key biological markers and health metrics to identify any deviations from the individual's normal baseline. When these markers start deviating, it signifies a transition phase from wellness to disease, what Hood refers to as the earliest transition into the disease, or "stage zero." At this point, the disease has not fully developed and may not be diagnosable with traditional medical tests, but early signs of the disease process may be detectable with sensitive monitoring tools.

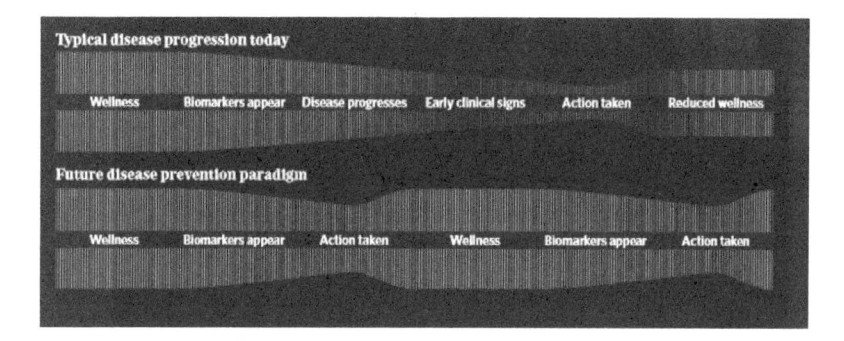

Leroy Hood's Disease Progression Today[75]

Next comes the disease phase, where symptoms appear and the disease can be diagnosed and treated with conventional medicine. This is typically where most of our health care interventions occur today. However, according to Hood's model, the goal of modern health care should be to detect and intervene at the transition phase or even earlier, during the wellness phase, using personalized, predictive, and preventive strategies. This approach aims to keep individuals in the wellness phase for as long as possible, delaying the onset of diseases or, ideally, preventing them entirely: stage zero health care! Patients would then be empowered to prevent what they can and prepare for what they cannot.

This model emphasizes the importance of comprehensive data collection, including genomic, phenomic, lifestyle, and environmental

---

[75] https://www.scientificamerican.com/custom-media/the-new-science-of-wellness/.

factors, as well as the use of big data analytics and AI to predict and prevent diseases. It also highlights the importance of patient participation in their own health, such as self-monitoring and making lifestyle adjustments based on personalized health insights. In summary, Hood's typical disease and wellness progression model presents a forward-thinking approach to health care, aiming to shift our focus from disease treatment to disease prevention and wellness maintenance. It highlights the potential for digital technologies, such as wearables and AI, to transform health care delivery, making it more proactive, predictive, personalized, and participatory.

Most general wellness programs tend to focus on nutrition, physical activity, stress, and sleep, which are all proven methods to improve health and prevent disease. The difference with scientific wellness is that it approaches these same interventions with a rigorous, data-driven mindset. The ultimate goal for doctors, medical device manufacturers, pharmaceutical companies, hospitals, insurance companies, and other health care organizations is to help each of us lead a longer, healthier life. But at present, incentives in the industry put too much emphasis on treatment and not enough on wellness and prevention. Only about 3 percent of the $4 trillion spent by the US medical industry is currently spent on prevention.[76]

The scientific approach to achieving stage zero health care is personalized care that spots the earliest signs of disease and intervenes to stop it from developing. The science and technology to help us predict and prevent diseases is arriving. The big task now is to make it work for millions of people. Delivering targeted interventions to achieve zero stage health care of millions of people requires translating scientific discoveries into a prevention and wellness industry. A person might inherit a gene for cancer, for example, but diet, medication, and exercise changes can lower the chance that cancer will develop. This requires detailed snapshots of their genes (what's coded in DNA), but also other major factors that predispose us to either wellness or disease, including their body's gut bacteria (microbiome), proteins, and other biomarkers, as well as their

---

[76] https://www.scientificamerican.com/custom-media/the-new-science-of-wellness/evidence-based-wellness-emerges-as-an-industry/.

life history, nutrition, and environment. This integrated picture is the phenome, and in recent years, a wave of startup digital health companies have begun to offer aspects of what could eventually grow into an ecosystem of businesses and organizations that provide all the steps in the process of keeping each of us healthy and detecting disease at stage zero. These steps include administering tests that yield data relevant to an individual's state of wellness, interpreting that data, and providing safe and effective interventions to stave off disease. These interventions can be as simple as making it easier for people to choose foods that help them maintain their health, rather than sugary drinks and fries, as well as more targeted actions such as optimizing levels of a vitamin or administering a drug. Unlike much of the current prevention and wellness industry, these interventions must be rooted in science, personalized to the individual and trackable in a way that makes it possible to measure the results over time. We use longitudinal phenomics—a holistic approach to collecting data on our phenome over time. This allows us to build a comprehensive digital image of our health and the factors that influence it. Our life and health are dynamic, so we benefit from identifying how our phenome changes in response to our lifestyle and environment changes.

Although the scientific wellness industry is still in its infancy, a great deal of progress has been made in all three areas: testing, interpreting, and intervening. Arivale[77] was launched in 2015 with the vision of making personalized, data-driven, preventive coaching a new wellness paradigm in the United States. The Arivale program collected dense data clouds of information for each participant over time, including genomic, blood analytes, gut microbiome, and digital self-measurements. Based on this data and systems and behavioral science, Arivale health coaches presented participants with a personalized list of recommendations for improving their wellness and avoiding disease. Despite remarkable success, they had to regrettably terminate their consumer program in 2019 due to the simple fact that the cost of providing the service exceeds what their customers could pay for it. They believe the costs of collecting the genetic, blood, and microbiome assays that form the

---

[77] http://www.arivale.com/.

foundation of the program will eventually decline to a point where the program can be delivered to consumers cost-effectively.

We are all more than a single data point. Our genes, behavior, and environment work together to produce our phenome—the continuously changing representation of our biology. We can understand our phenome by looking at biological samples like our blood, gut microbes, and DNA, or lifestyle habits such as how much we exercise and our dietary patterns. Genetic testing provides a fundamental basis from which to guide personalized scientific prevention and wellness. Ancestry,[78] 23andme,[79] and other firms have now performed genetic tests for more than 30 million people, providing insights into genetic predisposition to diseases, how well an individual metabolizes caffeine, and more. Many companies provide health advice based on genomics. For instance, 3x4 Genetics[80] produces genetic reports intended to be interpreted with guidance from a physician. And Self Decode[81] provides personalized diet and lifestyle plans, informed by genetics, directly to consumers, or included in comprehensive health programs.

We now also have the ability to screen for thousands of genetic diseases in newborns. Advances in the speed of genetic sequencing and steeply falling costs have made it possible to screen for hundreds or even thousands of childhood-onset genetic diseases. Now 193 illnesses can be identified through DNA itself, using one of the more popular commercial genetic test panels for newborns, Sema4's Natalis. Natalis screens for diseases that are treatable. A total of 1,514 genes, each responsible for a different childhood disease, were identified in a research study on newborns called BabySeq. It looked for DNA tied to treatable illnesses, for genes that can affect responses to drugs, and for genes that would not affect the particular baby but could be passed on and cause disease in future generations. And companies such as Sema4 and BabyGenes are now marketing 23andMe-style direct-to consumer tests to parents simply seeking to know more about the health of their baby.

---

[78] https://www.ancestry.com/dna/.
[79] https://www.23andme.com/dna-health-ancestry/.
[80] https://3x4genetics.com/.
[81] https://selfdecode.com/.

Out gut microbiome—the unique mix of microbes in each person's digestive tract—plays a role in asthma, diabetes, Parkinson's disease, and other conditions. That mix, detectable from stool samples, is influenced by genetics, diet, stress, and environmental exposures, such as what an infant encounters in the birth canal. Thorne[82] recently developed a "microbiome wipe" that makes collecting a stool sample as easy as using toilet paper, replacing the old "poop and scoop" approach that consumers dislike.

Metabolites and proteins offer powerful clues to the underlying biochemical activity in the human body. This in turn can yield signs of impending disease long before symptoms appear. Startups are bringing testing now available only in labs or in the doctor's office to the individual. (See "Zero Wait.") Blood samples can now be collected at home simply, and nearly painlessly, with devices such as the OneDraw or Tasso. Blood based and digital diagnostics can track disease risk factors, such as hemoglobin (HbA1c), LDL and HDL cholesterol, thyroid markers, and hormone levels. Some startups are now offering products to make more effective use of data from these standard tests. Inside Tracker,[83] WellnessFx,[84] and others use these kinds of biomarkers to provide personalized insights into nutrition and lifestyle choices.

Social and lifestyle data includes nutrition, exercise, and stress—things that a fitness tracking device can collect. The Apple Watch, Fitbit, and other products now provide information on activity, sleep, heart rate variability, and more. Other measures like blood pressure, heart rate, and other vital signs fall in this catchall category. Such data can be integrated across many devices through Apple Health or CommonHealth on Android phones. This category also includes environmental exposures, past traumas, and other historical events that impact a person's health. These would be captured by surveys and screenings. Other data that is gathered in a clinical setting, such as MRIs, and electronic health records, are also important.

---

[82] https://thorne.com.
[83] https://www.insidetracker.com/.
[84] https://www.wellnessfx.com/.

Implementing a zero stage health care model with the support of technologies like whole body scanning can also transform health outcomes significantly. By detecting diseases at their earliest, most treatable stages, this approach could reduce the burden of chronic diseases, increase the effectiveness of treatments, and improve patients' quality of life. Prenuvo,[85] a Silicon Valley startup has pioneered the conceptive zero stage whole body scanning. Neko health[86] is a preventative health care technology that has developed a new medical scanning technology concept to make it possible to do broad and noninvasive health data collection that is quick, convenient, and affordable ($250). After it first launched earlier this year in Stockholm, Sweden, Neko Health sold out all the slots in less than two hours. And the enthusiasm for its preventative approach to health care remains high with over 10,000 people currently on the waiting list and a rebooking rate of 80 percent after the initial scan. This shows that the vast majority of its members choose to make this part of their annual health routine.[87]

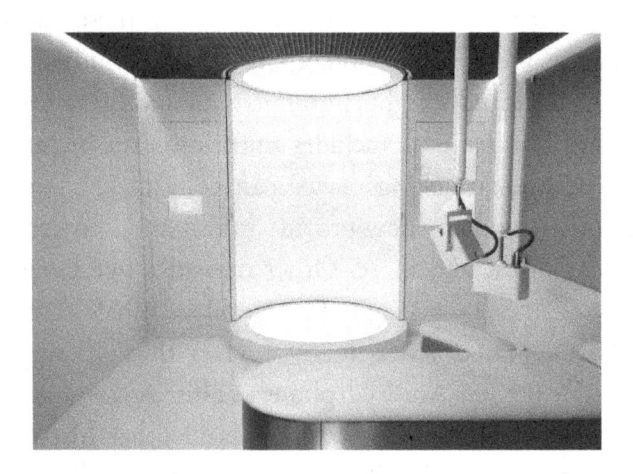

Neko Body Scan[88]

---

[85] https://www.prenuvo.com/.
[86] https://www.nekohealth.com/en.
[87] https://pulse2.com/neko-health-e60-million-funding/.
[88] https://www.nekohealth.com/en/scan.

By paying close attention to brain health and intervening at the first sign of trouble, most neurological and psychiatric illnesses may be preventable. Even though a majority of people are challenged by a life-degrading neurological or psychiatric illness across a significant span of their lives, there's no equivalent of a stethoscope, blood pressure cuff, or EKG to routinely assess brain health during a visit to the doctor. Professor Mike Merzenich, an outstanding neurophysiologist, has pioneered the idea of brain health and plasticity throughout life, and the assessment and management of brain health through digital measurements of forty different types that assess twenty-five different cognitive features (e.g., reaction time, peripheral field vision, and memory).[89] He demonstrated that on average a person's cognitive abilities increase to a maximum at thirty-five years of age and thereafter, for most of us, decline throughout the rest of our lives. In a clinical trial with ten eighty-year-old individuals, Professor Merzenich was able to demonstrate that with brain training, they could be brought back to the cognitive capacities they should have had in their midthirties. Thus, the brain is plastic through life and many of us have the potential to largely retain our optimal cognitive functions with digitally driven brain practice. Dr. Merzenich started the company Posit (now BrainHQ)[90] to deliver brain health to individuals. He has carried out more than 250 successful clinical trials with more than 10,000 individuals to demonstrate the effectiveness of his cognitive training approach to brain health in dealing with health optimization for cognitively normal individuals and in dealing with certain brain diseases.

Muse[91] is a brain sensing headband that uses EEG technology to track your brain activity, heart rate, and breath. It can be used for meditation, sleep tracking, and biofeedback and is a safe and effective tool for brain health that has tested and validated by neuroscientists. It improves your focus and concentration, which can be helpful for people who struggle with attention deficit hyperactivity disorder

---

[89] https://www.congress.gov/117/meeting/house/114289/witnesses/HHRG-117-IF14-Wstate-HoodL-20211208.pdf.

[90] https://www.brainhq.com/.

[91] https://choosemuse.com/.

(ADHD) or anxiety, it reduces stress and anxiety, helpful for people who experience chronic stress or anxiety disorders, and improves sleep, which can be helpful for people who have trouble sleeping or who suffer from insomnia. Muse headbands also track your progress over time so you can see how your brain activity changes as you meditate or sleep. This can help you stay motivated and see the benefits of using Muse headband.

Openwater[92] is developing a portable, wearable therapeutic and diagnostic headset that may be capable of treating cancer, mental disease, and measuring features related to cerebral blood flow. Their technology is noninvasive, low-cost, and portable and may allow for broader applications including point of care. Hospital studies are underway for potential future uses, including treatment of cancer, mental disease, neurodegenerative disease, and early precision stroke detection and routing, which could save hundreds of millions of lives.

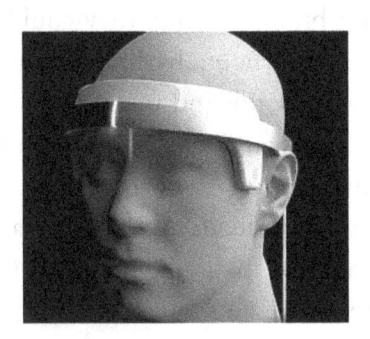

Openwater Wearable MRI[93]

The next step in zero stage medicine is to turn the above testing data into meaningful insights that can enhance wellness and help each of us to work toward health goals. The two main ways of gaining this insight are through human experts and guided AI—or, more commonly, a combination of both. The key objective is to make the observations actionable for individuals.

---

[92] https://www.openwater.cc/.
[93] https://www.openwater.cc/products.

The concept of biological age is a measure of how old your body is at a cellular level, as opposed to your chronological age. It is determined by a variety of factors, including your genes, lifestyle choices, and environment. While chronological age is a good predictor of health and longevity, biological age is far more accurate indicator. Understanding one's biological age can provide a clearer picture of their overall health and wellness, serving as a valuable tool for stage zero intervention. For instance, someone might have a chronological age of forty but a biological age of thirty-five due to a healthy lifestyle and good genetics. Conversely, a person might be chronologically thirty but have a biological age of forty due to poor lifestyle choices or certain environmental factors. Several models and biomarkers, including telomere length, epigenetic alterations, and molecular changes, are used to estimate biological age. Advanced techniques, such as artificial intelligence and machine learning, are also used to integrate these diverse data points and provide a comprehensive estimate of biological age. Here's how the concept of biological age can be applied to prevention and wellness:

- *early detection and prevention.* Biological age can be used to detect early signs of aging and disease, which can be useful for preventive measures. For instance, individuals with a higher biological age might be encouraged to adopt healthier lifestyle habits to lower their risk of age-related diseases.
- *tailored interventions.* Knowing one's biological age allows for personalized health interventions. For example, people with a higher biological age could benefit from more aggressive interventions, such as a stricter exercise routine, diet changes, stress management techniques, or even pharmaceutical intervention.
- *monitoring and evaluation.* Biological age can also serve as a measure to evaluate the effectiveness of health interventions. Changes in biological age over time can help track the progress of interventions and adjust them as necessary.
- *research and understanding aging.* On a larger scale, the concept of biological age contributes to our understanding of the aging

process, which could lead to breakthroughs in anti-aging research and longevity medicine.

Many companies are also developing tools to interpret data and suggest personalized actions to improve health. Some focus on behavioral change, such as Levels and Noom. Others, such as Thorne HealthTech and DayTwo, interpret microbiome tests to make recommendations about lifestyle, diet, and nutrition. Other firms, such as January.ai and NutriSense, provide insights based on continuous glucose-monitoring data. Apps such as Welltory and Humanity integrate digital health data to provide insights. An exciting development is the use of a "digital twin" as an in silico representation of an individual's specific biology. In principle, clinicians or companies can use them to make predictions of the effects of interventions on the individual and represent the variability of response across large populations. The combination of digital twins that represent individual biology with machine learning from patient data provides a powerful approach to deciphering the complexity of wellness and disease.

As we conclude our examination of technology's impact on zero stage medicine, specifically within the context of P4 (predictive, preventive, personalized, and participatory) medicine, several key takeaways emerge. First, advancements in technology have proven instrumental in elevating P4 medicine to unprecedented levels. Not only has technology allowed us to expand our ability to predict and prevent diseases, but it has also vastly improved our capacity to personalize and participate in our own health management.

Artificial intelligence, big data analytics, machine learning, genomics, and wearable technology have dramatically transformed our ability to forecast disease risks, thereby enabling health care providers to administer preventive measures at the zero stage—before diseases fully manifest. These technologies help to create personalized health plans that are uniquely tailored to an individual's genetic makeup, lifestyle, and environmental factors. Furthermore, the evolution of digital health platforms has empowered patients to actively participate in their own health care. Health-tracking applications, telemedicine, and virtual health care consultations are all examples of this shift toward patient-centered, participatory medicine. They not only provide real-time monitoring and feedback but also foster an enhanced understanding of personal health dynamics, fostering more informed decisions.

Secondly, while the benefits are profound, there are still significant challenges that lie ahead. Data privacy and ethical considerations, the digital divide, and the need for further research and standardization in implementing these technologies are all areas that need careful attention. As we embrace these new technologies, it's crucial that we ensure they are used ethically, responsibly, and inclusively. The safety threshold for intervening in otherwise healthy people is much higher than for treating people who are already sick. This puts a burden on wellness and prevention companies more akin to food companies than those in the pharmaceutical or medical device industries. Precision interventions to improve healthy aging require a higher safety threshold than interventions developed for late-stage disease. For this reason, prevention and wellness won't use the kind of drugs aimed primarily at late-stage disease. Implementing an intervention with serious side effects might be warranted and chosen for someone with a serious disease, but clearly not with individuals who are for the most part healthy. This means we need to develop interventions that can be deployed with specificity and with low or no side effects. Although particularly safe drugs show promise for use in wellness and to improve aging, metformin, for instance, is currently under study in the Targeting Aging with Metformin trial led by Nir Barzalai, the head of the Institute for Aging Research at the Albert Einstein College of Medicine and scientific director for the American Federation for Aging Research. Many of these targeted interventions are likely to come from natural products guided by testing and personalized insights. Of course, just because something is in the natural world doesn't necessarily make it safe, and nutraceuticals (nutrients that can also be used as medicines) can have strong biological effects. But the focus should be on those natural products that the Food and Drug Administration can categorize as "Generally Recognized as Safe" (GRAS) or those that can be submitted to the FDA for classification as a new dietary ingredient.

The power of zero stage medicine lies not just in its potential to transform how we detect and treat disease but also in its capacity to shift the collective mindset toward health and wellness. The potential for technology to revolutionize zero stage medicine and P4 medicine as a whole is undeniable. It provides a vision for a future where disease is not just managed but prevented, where medicine is not generalized but personalized, and where patients are not merely passive recipients but active participants in their own health care journey. Thus, we find ourselves at the frontier of a health care transformation that can usher in an era of unprecedented patient empowerment, disease prevention, and wellness optimization. The role of technology in enabling this transformation is both pivotal and indisputable. As we move forward, it will be essential to continue exploring and harnessing the full potential of these technologies while always remembering to maintain a human-centered approach to health care.

As we close this chapter, we look ahead with anticipation and a sense of responsibility. Digital health technology offers us an unprecedented opportunity to revolutionize health care, making zero stage medicine a reality. As we continue our journey toward perfect health care, let's embrace these tools and the potential they hold while staying mindful of the challenges they present. The journey toward zero stage medicine is indeed a journey toward the very essence of P4 medicine—a health system that is predictive, preventive, personalized, and participatory. This pursuit is more than just an evolution; it's a revolution in health care.

ZERO EXCLUSION

AS WE EMBARK on the next stage of our journey to zero, we examine an aspect of health care that is often overlooked but critically important: the goal of zero exclusion. Inclusion and equity in health care are fundamental rights, not mere privileges. Yet disparities persist across various dimensions, such as race, socioeconomic status, geography, and disability, leading to exclusion and unequal health outcomes.

Digital health technology has the potential to both exacerbate and alleviate these disparities. On one hand, the advent of digital health could unintentionally create a "digital divide" where only certain populations have access to or can benefit from technological advances, thereby further widening health disparities. On the other hand, if implemented thoughtfully and inclusively, digital health could democratize access to health care, provide personalized care solutions, and ultimately drive us toward the goal of zero exclusion.

In this chapter, we will examine the complex and dual role of digital health technology in addressing health disparities. We'll explore the risks it poses in widening the digital divide and the incredible potential it holds to bridge these gaps. Through a series of case studies, insights, challenges, and opportunities, we will discuss how digital health technology can be used to achieve zero exclusion in health care. The pursuit of zero exclusion medicine represents a commitment to making health care accessible, equitable, and personalized for all, irrespective of their circumstances. It is a journey that requires us to view digital health technology not just as a tool for improved health care but as a means to ensure justice and fairness in health care access and outcomes.

So let's delve into this important aspect of our journey to zero, where we explore the promise and challenges of utilizing digital health technology to attain true inclusivity in health care.

Today, access to computing devices and the internet, and the skill to use both, is essential to all aspects of life. The use of digital tools and applications is steadily increasing and can support a range of health information needs. As tools such as patient portals, health trackers, and remote monitoring devices see greater use, research suggests that tools such as health apps and patient portals can foster greater patient engagement, better support patients outside of the clinic visit, and can improve health outcomes. However, greater reliance on digital tools has the potential to increase disparities between those who have skills and access to digital tools and those who do not and thereby existing health disparities.

A World Economic Forum[94] report suggests a shocking state of global internet connectivity. A decent internet connection—essential for many basic tasks in the COVID-19 era—is out of reach for 90 per cent of people in low- and middle-income countries. While just under half of people in low- and middle-income countries have access to basic internet connectivity, this is not adequate for them to access essential health, education, and employment services. According to a recent Brookings Institution report,[95] 15–24 percent of Americans lack any sort of broadband connection to the internet with which to use mobile health technology. These differences only increase when examining the issue by income groups: 38 percent of households earning less than $20,000 lack a broadband subscription. The digital divide by income exists in both rural and urban areas.

Digital literacies and internet connectivity have been called the "super social determinants of health" because they address all other social determinants of health (SDOH). For example, applications for employment, housing, and other assistance programs, each of which influences an individual's health, are increasingly, and sometimes exclusively, accessible online. The costs of equipping a person to use

---

[94] https://www.weforum.org/agenda/2022/03/reliable-internet-unavailable-poorest-global-population/.

[95] Tomer, A., Fishbane, L., Siefer, A., Callahan, B. Digital Prosperity: How Broadband Can Deliver Health and Equity to All Communities. (Metropolitan Infrastructure Initiative: Brookings Institution, 2020).

the internet are substantially lower than treating health conditions and the benefits are persistent and significant, making the efforts to improve digital literacy skills and access valuable tools to reduce disparities.

About 2.9 billion people—over a third of the world's population—have never used the internet. Most of these are found in East Asia, South Asia, the Pacific Islands, the Caribbean, and Africa. They are digitally excluded because of various challenges including poverty, lack of digital skills, lack of electricity, and geographical challenges.[96]

Men are also 21 percent more likely to be online than women globally, rising to 52 percent in least developed countries. Various barriers prevent women and girls from accessing the internet and participating online, including unaffordable devices and data tariffs, inequalities in education and digital skills, social norms that discourage women and girls from being online, and fears around privacy, safety, and security. While digital exclusion limits the opportunities for those women and girls unable to connect, it also has broader societal and economic impacts that affect everyone. With hundreds of millions fewer women able to use the internet, the world is missing out on untold social, cultural, and economic contributions that they could make if they were able to harness the internet's benefits. A digital economy without the full participation of women cannot scale to reach its potential. Digital inclusion is not only good policy but also good economics.

Over a billion people globally, approximately 15 percent of the world's population, have disabilities and 80 percent of them live in developing countries. More than 40 million people in the United States have a disability. The Pew[97] report revealed the extent to which people with disabilities are still on the sidelines of the digital revolution. Fifty-four percent of households with a disability use the internet, compared to 81 percent of households with no disability in the United States. Also, as majorities of these Americans report having certain technologies, the digital divide between those who have a disability and those who

---

[96] https://www.weforum.org/agenda/2022/03/reliable-internet-unavailable-poorest-global-population/.

[97] https://www.pewresearch.org/internet/2012/08/06/disability-in-the-digital-age/.

do not remains for some devices. Some 62 percent of adults with a disability say they own a desktop or laptop computer, compared with 81 percent of those without a disability, according to a Pew Research Center survey of US adults conducted from January 25 to February 8, 2021. And when it comes to smartphone ownership, there is a gap of 16 percentage points between those with a disability and those without one (72 percent versus 88 percent).[98]

Everyone deserves an equal opportunity to benefit from health technology. The digital divide in health care highlights our failure to adapt tools and provide the support people need to maximize use of the technology they already have. At a time when access to technology and the internet is higher than ever, it is imperative we pivot to provide the technology support the underserved need. If we are ever to achieve health equity, this pivot is essential.

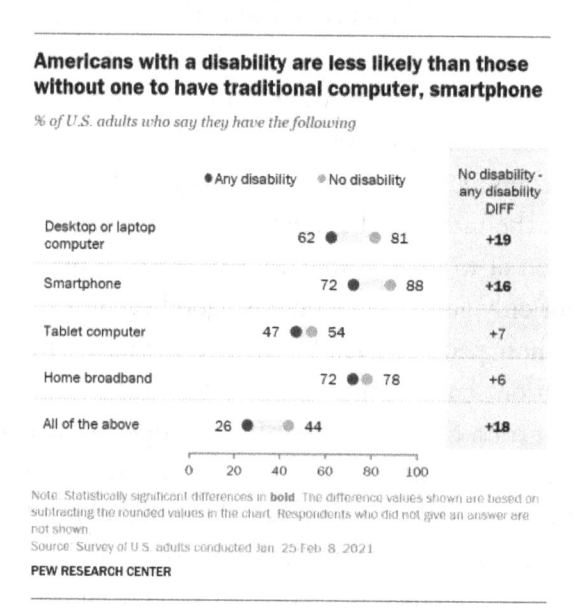

Americans with a disability are less likely than those without one to have traditional computer, smartphone

% of U.S. adults who say they have the following

	Any disability	No disability	No disability - any disability DIFF
Desktop or laptop computer	62	81	+19
Smartphone	72	88	+16
Tablet computer	47	54	+7
Home broadband	72	78	+6
All of the above	26	44	+18

Note: Statistically significant differences in **bold**. The difference values shown are based on subtracting the rounded values in the chart. Respondents who did not give an answer are not shown.
Source: Survey of U.S. adults conducted Jan. 25-Feb. 8, 2021

PEW RESEARCH CENTER

With these challenges in mind, we offer recommendations. *First,* health care systems should adopt a digital inclusion-informed strategy regarding mobile health that recognizes their community's level of

---

[98] https://www.pewresearch.org/short-reads/2021/09/10/americans-with-disabilities-less-likely-than-those-without-to-own-some-digital-devices/.

access to devices and internet connectivity and supports patients in their initial and sustained technology use. Digital inclusion refers to the activities necessary to ensure equitable access to and use of information and communication technologies, including affordable broadband internet service, internet-enabled devices, access to digital literacy training, quality technical support, and applications and online content designed to enable and encourage self-sufficiency, participation, and collaboration. These form the foundation for use of mobile technology in health care. While knowing whether an individual's access is important, it is vital for health systems to understand the larger environment shaping patients' digital experience. Adoption rates are nearing ubiquity among highly educated individuals with at least moderate income, but important pockets of nonadoption remain.

Most mobile health technology requires a data plan and/or home broadband, yet the American Community Survey shows that 40 percent of low-income households lack a subscription, requiring them to use limited cell plan data or local public Wi-Fi hotspots. These options may appear affordable, but they contain important limitations. Using prepaid plans, patients may run out of data or need to prioritize data for specific uses. Even with their lower cost, they may still be unaffordable, particularly for families in need of multiple devices. Open Wi-Fi access points are another option but may only be available in public locations in which patients may feel uncomfortable accessing their personal health information.

Prior to the rapid increase in telehealth use due to COVID-19, patient portals to their EHR were the most common form of mobile health and a gateway to other mobile health applications. However, studies show that lack of internet access is a leading factor inhibiting use of patient portals. Smartphones may seem to be a logical and ubiquitous substitute for home internet, but significant gaps still exist for rural, poor, and older adults. Research shows that nearly half of older adults and 30 percent of those earning less than $30,000 own a smartphone and many low-income households share devices, raising both access and privacy issues. Understanding the nuances of access in the communities they serve can help health care systems implement more inclusive strategies.

Digitally inclusive strategies of health system adoption also support patients in their use of technology at all levels and should include digital skills training, particularly for recent adopters of technology or those who may have devices with limited features. Patients may also need assistance with setting up email and patient portal accounts. In addition, it is critical to provide ongoing support for patients, reduce medical jargon, provide interpretive resources, and ensure that technology and training are offered equitably to all patients, not just to those who are confident enough to request help.

Second, we recommend systematically assessing individual patients' access and digital literacies. This became particularly clear since the rapid and pervasive shift to telehealth during the COVID-19 pandemic. Simply asking patients what devices they own and how they access the internet is not typical in the clinical context, but this information can shape the type of technology a clinician can recommend. The lack of routine assessment prior to COVID-19 meant that some patients fell between the cracks as care shifted to nearly all virtual. Incorporating this and other SDOH into the EHR encourages more consistent documentation and allows assessment of population-level metrics of access. When digital skill and connectivity gaps are assessed systematically and universally, a health system can document overall population-level metrics, examine disparities, and track changes over time.

Third, health systems should partner with community organizations with expertise in training in digital literacy skills and facilitating connectivity. Libraries not only offer the internet but also provide a spectrum of training services from basic digital literacies to skills required for specific devices and applications. Some communities have leveraged community health workers and patient navigators to screen and refer patients for gaps in basic digital literacies and connectivity. They can provide hands-on training in the use of mobile health technologies for patients who do have adequate digital access. Allied health professional education programs leverage a "train the trainer" model to prepare the future health care workforce to undertake these tasks. The National Digital Inclusion Alliance (NDIA) offers a comprehensive list of organizations across the country that provide digital literacy training and national and local resources for free/low-cost internet and computers.

Mobile health technologies hold significant promise to increase the efficiency of care and improve health outcomes. Yet we must be cognizant of their potential to increase health disparities. National efforts have been undertaken to promote broadband, such as the Federal Communications Commission's (FCC) Lifeline Program that subsidizes the cost of smartphones and internet service for low-income individuals. However, the Lifeline Program's impact is limited by low consumer awareness, and the qualification process varies by state and by the service provider. The new bipartisan infrastructure law (Infrastructure Investment and Jobs Act) is making the Affordable Connectivity Program, originally called the Emergency Broadband Benefit, a permanent program for those who cannot afford internet. The initiative will provide households that meet certain income level thresholds to earn $30 per month toward their connectivity costs. As clinical care incorporates more technology in more contexts, we suggest the recommendations above to facilitate equitable adoption of mobile health technology.

Digital health technology developers have a responsibility to ensure that their products are accessible to everyone, regardless of their background, abilities, or location. This means considering a wide range of factors during the product development process, from the design of the product to the way it is marketed and supported.

Here are some of the key things that digital health technology developers need to consider in order to achieve zero exclusion:

- *improve accessibility.* Make sure that digital platforms are accessible to all, following the principles of universal design. This includes providing alternative text for images, subtitles for videos, and assistive technologies, such as screen readers and voice controls. The product must be available in multiple languages. This ensures that people from all over the world can access the product. This means taking into account factors such as internet access, cultural differences, and regulatory requirements of other countries as well. Companies like HealthTap have integrated automated translation services, making it accessible to non-English speakers. Google has made its Translate app available in over one hundred languages.

- affordable assistive technologies. Many individuals with disabilities rely on assistive technologies like screen readers, alternative keyboards, or specialized software to access digital content. The product must be affordable for people from all income levels. This may involve offering free or low-cost versions of the product or providing financial assistance to people who need it. Making these tools more affordable and widely available can significantly bridge the gap. Companies like mySugr offer their basic app for free, providing millions of people with diabetes a tool to manage their condition better. The WHO has developed a number of free and low-cost digital health tools, such as the mHealth Toolkit and the Mental Health Gap Action Programme.
- *integration with existing systems.* Digital health tools should be designed to integrate smoothly with existing health care systems. This can help promote wider adoption and usage. For example, Zocdoc integrates with existing health records and insurance providers to streamline the appointment scheduling process.
- *data privacy.* Ensuring the privacy and security of health data is crucial. A breach of data privacy can disproportionately impact disadvantaged groups. Thus, companies should adhere to stringent data protection standards. Apple's HealthKit platform, for instance, places a strong emphasis on protecting user data.
- *inclusive design practices.* Tech companies should involve individuals with disabilities in the design process to ensure that their needs are met. This is sometimes referred to as "nothing about us without us." It's essential to understand

the specific challenges faced by people with different types of disabilities to create more inclusive technology. Companies like PatientsLikeMe incorporate user feedback into the development process to ensure their platforms are truly user centric.
- *addressing specific needs of underserved populations.* Certain groups face unique health challenges that are often overlooked. Developers can address this by designing targeted solutions for these groups. Butterfly Network's handheld, affordable ultrasound device, for instance, is specifically designed to address diagnostic challenges in remote areas and low-resource settings.
- *education and training.* There is a need to educate both those with disabilities and the wider population about digital technologies and their usage. This includes training individuals with disabilities to use assistive technologies and educating developers and designers about how to create accessible digital content.
- *public policy.* Work closely with governments and policymakers who can play a crucial role in bridging the disability digital divide. They can enact and enforce laws ensuring digital accessibility, fund programs to provide assistive technologies to those who need them, and incorporate digital accessibility into public education curriculums. In many areas, individuals with disabilities may also struggle with access to reliable, high-speed internet, particularly in rural or lower-income regions. Efforts should be made to improve the infrastructure necessary for internet access in these areas.
- *partnerships.* Work with NGOs to drive change. This could include initiatives to develop more accessible technologies, programs to get assistive devices to those who need them, and campaigns to raise awareness about the importance of digital accessibility. There is also a need to educate both those with disabilities and the wider population about digital technologies and their usage. This includes training individuals with

disabilities to use assistive technologies and educating developers and designers about how to create accessible digital content.

There are numerous companies that are doing a good job of considering these factors in their product development. For example, Apple is a great example of building into its products accessibility features aimed at users with disabilities. These groundbreaking features were designed with feedback from members of disability communities every step of the way, to support a diverse set of users and help people connect in new ways. These can be reviewed at https://support.apple.com/accessibility. By considering these factors, digital health technology developers can help to ensure that their products are accessible to everyone, regardless of their background, abilities, or location. This is essential for creating a more inclusive and equitable health care system. In addition to the factors mentioned above, digital health technology developers should also consider the following:

- the needs of the target audience. Who is the product being developed for? What are their specific needs and challenges?
- the context of use. How will the product be used? What are the environmental and social factors that need to be considered?
- the ethical implications. What are the ethical considerations of developing and using this product? How can the product be used in a way that respects people's privacy and autonomy?

By taking all of these factors into account, digital health technology developers can create products that are truly inclusive and accessible to everyone—true democratization of health care where exclusion is a thing of the past.

Artificial Intelligence can make health care more accessible to underserved groups, but it also risks reinforcing existing inequities because AI models can perpetuate biases lurking in the data. Medical AI systems can fail to generalize to new kinds of data they were not trained on; thus, training on datasets that underrepresent marginalized groups is well known to result in biased systems that underperform on those groups. Systems that explicitly factor race into their predictions are also at risk of perpetuating prejudice, because racial categories are difficult to define and obscure the diversity within racial groups. Bias can creep in due to other design choices, such as the choice of target label. For example, a risk-assessment algorithm used to guide clinical decision-making for 200 million patients was found to give racially biased predictions, such that White patients assigned a certain predicted risk score tended to be healthier than Black patients with the same score did. This bias was due in large part to the original labels used in training. The system was trained to predict future health care costs, but because Black patients had historically received less expensive care than White patients due to existing systematic biases, the system reproduced those racial biases in its predictions.[99] Extensive research is necessary to detect and correct bias in medical AI models because bias can cause widespread harm to marginalized groups if left unchecked. In the future, AI tools may systematically undergo special testing before deployment to verify that neural networks serve the well-being of marginalized populations equitably. Additionally, it may become easier to identify dangerous bias if model explainability improves because human monitors will be able to double-check the reasoning of AI systems and identify problematic elements.

As we conclude this chapter, the dual nature of digital health in shaping disparities becomes abundantly clear. Digital health technology, in its transformative power, holds the capacity to both cause and resolve disparities, highlighting the thin line that separates inclusivity from exclusion. The world of digital health can indeed be a double-edged sword. In the absence of thoughtful design and purposeful implementation, it may exacerbate existing disparities, creating a digital divide that only widens the chasm of inequality. It may favor those with resources and knowledge, leaving behind those who are most vulnerable and further marginalizing them in a realm that should ideally be their

---

[99] Obermeyer, Z., Powers, B., Vogeli, C. & Mullainathan, S. Dissecting racial bias in an algorithm used to manage the health of populations. Science 366, 447–453 (2019).

refuge: health care. Yet on the flip side, when designed and deployed with inclusivity, equity, and accessibility at its core, digital health technology can be a beacon of hope and an enabler of change. It can break down barriers, erase boundaries, and ensure that no individual, no community, no population is left behind in the pursuit of health and wellness. It can ensure that health care, in its most advanced and personalized form, is not a privilege but a right accessible by all.

As we have explored in this chapter, this zero exclusion approach is not a distant dream but an attainable reality. Digital health companies that focus on accessibility, affordability, cultural relevance, system integration, underserved needs, data privacy, and user involvement in design are already carving the path toward it. The journey to zero exclusion is a commitment to equality in its truest sense. It requires acknowledging that while disparities exist, they are not inevitable. It reminds us that technology, in its essence, is a tool, and like any tool, its impact—positive or negative—is defined by how we wield it.

As we continue this journey, the role of digital health technology will remain critical. The task ahead is to leverage it not as a divider but as a unifier, a bridge that connects us all in our shared pursuit of health. The journey toward zero exclusion in medicine is, indeed, a journey toward a more equitable, inclusive, and just health care system for all.

ZERO EMISSION

AS WE STEP into a new chapter in our journey to zero, we venture into a realm that converges health care with an issue of universal concern: environmental sustainability. The concept of zero emission is not typically associated with health care, but as the digital revolution permeates the sector, the link becomes increasingly significant. The health care sector, in its pursuit of saving lives, has a considerable environmental footprint. In fact, it is estimated that the health care sector accounts for around 4 percent of global greenhouse gas emissions, and according to Health Care Without Harm, if the global health care sector were a country, it would be the fifth-largest greenhouse gas emitter on the planet. In this context, digital health technologies emerge not only as a means to enhance health care but also as a tool to reduce its environmental impact.

However, like any other technology, digital health tools come with their own carbon footprint. The energy consumption of data centers, electronic waste from obsolete devices, and the impact of manufacturing new technology are just a few examples. Thus, the challenge is to leverage digital health technologies in a way that they contribute to zero emission in health care, rather than adding to the problem.

In this chapter, we will delve into the world of digital health through the lens of environmental sustainability. We'll explore the potential of these technologies to lower health care's environmental impact and discuss strategies for mitigating their own carbon footprints. From telemedicine reducing travel emissions to AI enabling energy-efficient diagnostics, we will examine a multitude of ways in which digital health can pave the way for a sustainable, zero emission health care system.

As we commence this journey, we keep in mind that the pursuit of zero emission in health care is not just about environmental sustainability. It represents a holistic approach to health, acknowledging that the health of individuals, communities, and the planet are interconnected. It underlines that as we strive for perfect health care, we must do so in a way that ensures a healthy planet for current and future generations. Join us as we embark on this crucial chapter in our quest for zero, discovering the role of digital health in sculpting a sustainable, zero emission health care landscape.

Digital health interventions are widely celebrated due to their low-cost nature and ability to provide tailored person-centered care in communities worldwide. Although interest in ethical questions surrounding digital health and issues of data sharing, security, privacy, and misinformation have increased, addressing such issues as the global environmental implications of digital health have been overlooked. In the US, health care accounts for 10 percent of the nation's carbon emissions (which make up 13.4 percent of all greenhouse gas emissions). By contrast, the aviation industry accounts for 2 percent of US carbon emissions. Considering climate change disproportionately affects the global south and global information and communication technology emissions already account for around 3.5 percent of global carbon emissions, the omission of environmental factors from digital health debates is significant. There is a pressing need to attend to the environmental impacts of digital health, understanding that in the long term, it can produce outcomes of ill health for the world's poorest and most vulnerable communities.

Younger clinicians who are coming of age now and starting to work in health care are passionate about the climate crisis. They see it for what it is, which is an existential threat and the greatest public health threat we face on the planet. There's a very powerful argument that phasing out fossil fuels will also be good for people's health. So there's a very strong health-based reason to address the climate crisis. Younger Americans—millennials and adults in Generation Z—stand out in a new Pew Research Center[100] survey, particularly for their high levels of engagement with the issue of climate change. Compared with

---

[100] https://www.pewresearch.org/science/2021/05/26/gen-z-millennials-stand-out-for-climate-change-activism-social-media-engagement-with-issue/.

older adults, Gen Zers and millennials are talking more about the need for action on climate change. Among social media users, they are seeing more climate change content online, and they are doing more to get involved with the issue through activities such as volunteering and attending rallies and protests. Digital engagement crosses age boundaries, but there are wide variations in the extent of use and the digital tools favored by age group. Gen Z engages in every type of digital health care activity more than other.[101]

The health care industry is increasingly addressing its contribution to climate change, and digital health technologies (DHT) may hold solutions to reducing health care's carbon footprint. For example, telehealth reduces transport-associated carbon emissions, fuel consumption, the consumption of paper, and personal protective equipment. However, DHT's benefits must be balanced against significant carbon impacts. Digital technology contributes to climate change and emissions in several ways, including the following:

- energy consumption. Digital technologies, particularly data centers and networks, consume significant amounts of energy. Data centers alone were estimated to account for about 1 percent of the global electricity use in 2020, according to the International Energy Agency (IEA). This energy often comes from fossil fuels, leading to greenhouse gas emissions.
- manufacturing process. The production of digital devices involves significant energy use and often generates considerable waste and pollution. The extraction and refining of rare earth elements and other materials used in these devices have significant environmental impacts.
- e-waste. E-waste, or electronic waste, is a rapidly growing problem. Many digital devices have short life spans and aren't recycled or disposed of properly, leading to environmental

---

[101] https://www.pymnts.com/study/connected-economy-omnichannel-healthcare-takes-center-stage-consumer-health-telehealth/?cache=skip#wpcf7-f1384772-o1?download=true.

pollution and wasted resources. E-waste can also leach hazardous materials into the environment if not managed properly.
- internet of things (IoT). As more devices become connected to the internet, the energy demand from these devices and the data they generate will also increase.
- cryptocurrencies. Certain digital technologies like cryptocurrencies, particularly Bitcoin, require immense computational power and therefore energy consumption. For instance, the process of Bitcoin mining consumes a lot of electricity, contributing to greenhouse gas emissions.
- artificial intelligence. The exact energy cost of a single AI model is difficult to estimate and includes the energy used to manufacture the computing equipment, create the model, and use the model in production. In 2019, researchers found that creating a generative AI model called BERT with 110 million parameters consumed the energy of a round-trip transcontinental flight for one person. The number of parameters refers to the size of the model, with larger models generally being more skilled. Researchers estimated that creating the much larger GPT-3, which has 175 billion parameters, consumed 1,287 megawatt hours of electricity and generated 552 tons of carbon dioxide equivalent, the equivalent of 123 gasoline-powered passenger vehicles driven for one year. And that's just for getting the model ready to launch, before any consumers start using it.

While a single large AI model is not going to ruin the environment, if a thousand companies develop slightly different AI bots for different purposes, each used by millions of customers, the energy use could become an issue. More research is needed to make generative AI more efficient. The good news is that AI can run on renewable energy. By bringing the computation to where green energy is more abundant, or scheduling computation for times of day when renewable energy is more available, emissions can be reduced by a factor of thirty to forty, compared to using a grid dominated by fossil fuels.

By choosing to implement DHTs with low carbon emission footprints, decision-makers will mitigate health care's carbon emissions and the impact of DHT on climate injustice that disproportionately affect vulnerable populations. Often obsolete information technology components (e-waste) are transported, treated, recycled, and destroyed in developing and impoverished nations. E-waste recycling processes may locally increase pollutants and toxins, impacting the health of those who are already vulnerable. Child labor is common in impoverished countries, potentially exposing children to toxic e-waste chemicals, linked to negative health outcomes, including cancer. Hence, there is an incentive to identify the best frameworks, methods, and tools to correctly identify DHTs with low carbon and other pollutant emissions.

Digital health technology developers and health systems can play a significant role in reducing emissions from the health care sector. Here are some specific ways they can contribute to zero emissions:

- They develop and deploy digital health solutions that reduce the need for travel. Remote patient monitoring, telehealth, and e-prescriptions are all examples of digital health solutions that can reduce the need for patients to travel to the doctor's office. This can save energy and reduce emissions. Developers should focus on creating robust, user-friendly telehealth solutions, and health systems should strive to integrate these solutions into their services.
- They design digital health solutions that are energy efficient. When designing digital health solutions, developers should consider the energy efficiency of the devices and software. For example, they can use energy-efficient hardware, such as low-power processors and displays or cloud-based solutions that reduce the need for on-site servers. They can also use energy-efficient software, such as algorithms that are optimized for performance and power consumption. Health systems, in turn, can opt for more energy-efficient digital solutions.
- They use renewable energy to power digital health infrastructure. When possible, digital health developers and health systems

should use renewable energy to power their infrastructure. This can include solar, wind, and hydroelectric power.
- They dispose of medical waste responsibly. Medical waste can be a major source of emissions. Developers should consider the entire life cycle of their products and create devices that are durable, recyclable, or upgradable. Health systems should partner with e-waste recycling organizations to responsibly dispose of obsolete equipment.
- AI and machine learning. These technologies can enhance the efficiency of health care delivery, reducing energy use and emissions. For example, AI algorithms can predict patient flow, helping hospitals operate more efficiently, or assist in diagnosis, reducing the need for repeat tests. Developers should continue to explore these AI applications, and health systems should invest in AI-integrated digital solutions.
- Digital records and paperless systems: Transitioning from paper to digital records can significantly reduce the environmental footprint of health systems. Digital health developers can aid in this transition by creating secure, accessible, and efficient EHR systems. Health systems can contribute by actively transitioning to paperless operations.
- Educating patients and staff: Both developers and health systems have a role in educating their users about the environmental impacts of health care and the benefits of digital health technologies in reducing this impact. This could include training on the responsible use and disposal of digital health devices.

By taking these steps, digital health technology developers and health systems can help to reduce emissions from the health care sector and contribute to a more sustainable future.

In addition to the specific actions listed above, digital health technology developers and health systems can also contribute to zero emissions by doing the following:

- supporting research on the environmental impact of digital health. There is still a lot that we don't know about the environmental impact of digital health. By supporting research in this area, we can better understand how to reduce the environmental impact of digital health solutions.
- involving patients and communities in the design of digital health solutions. Patients and communities can provide valuable insights into how to design digital health solutions that are both effective and sustainable. By involving patients and communities in the design process, we can ensure that digital health solutions meet the needs of all stakeholders.
- adopting a life cycle approach to sustainability. When designing and deploying digital health solutions, it is important to consider the entire life cycle of the solution, from the manufacturing of the devices to the disposal of the waste. By adopting a life cycle approach to sustainability, we can ensure that digital health solutions are truly sustainable.

Humane's AI Pin[102] is a wearable projector that flashes apps on hands or surfaces, functioning as a nonphysical smartphone. The connected and intelligent clothing-based wearable device uses a range of sensors that enable contextual and ambient compute interactions. The wearable smartphone and projector also functions as a voice assistant beyond web search and quick queries. It seems that it can also become a personal assistant reminding the user of their health issues and helping them with their indecisiveness when it comes to decisions concerning their health. This technology presents a huge opportunity for people to redefine their relationship to technology, and it will enable personal mobile computing to become faster, more powerful, and easier to use—and approach zero emission!

---

[102] https://hu.ma.ne/media/humane-names-first-device-humane-ai-pin.

Humane's Wearable Projector[103]

Finally, societal pressure may be helpful to encourage companies and research labs to publish the carbon footprints of their digital technologies and AI models, as some already do. In the future, perhaps consumers could even use this information to choose a "greener" technology or chatbot.

Digital health may have the potential to alleviate global health inequalities in the short term, but moving forward, there is a need to consider its long-term environmental sustainability. There must be an imperative to make environmental considerations a key priority when developing and implementing digital health. Building on the 2020 Riyadh Declaration on Digital Health, it is recommended that environmental audits of digital health interventions accounting for environmental impacts of devices, data and computation, and telehealth centers are carried out. Green information technologies and ethical sourcing and disposal of devices should be adopted where possible. However, there is also a need to lobby the digital technology field more broadly to ensure sustainable practices become standard, recognizing that many digital health technologies result from design and commercialization decisions beyond the field of health. Ensuring

---

[103] https://www.designboom.com/technology/humane-ai-pin-wearable-smartphone-project-apps-calls-hands-07-03-2023/.

environmental regulations are included in national and global health policy is thus essential to ensure big tech companies are incentivized to invest in more environmentally sustainable technologies. Without such steps, we risk that digital health will lead to additional global health burdens, creating ill health among the world's most vulnerable.

By creating digital health interventions that are environmentally sustainable through responsible design, development, and implementation, we have a real opportunity to make a difference. As demand from health care organizations for DHT increases, their collective market power to demand manufacturers publish transparent carbon emissions on DHT production must be used to support purchasing decisions. The shift by hospitals and private health care systems toward using DHTs to focus on disease prevention (rather than treatment) will reduce the need for carbon intensive treatment and facilities.

As we reach the close of this chapter, we recognize that the connection between digital health and environmental sustainability is both crucial and complex. As stewards of health, the responsibility of the health care sector extends beyond individual wellbeing to encompass the health of our planet. While the quest for zero emissions in health care is daunting, we have seen that digital health technologies can significantly contribute to this endeavor. From reducing the need for physical travel through telemedicine to promoting energy efficiency through AI and machine learning, digital health offers an array of promising pathways to diminish health care's carbon footprint. However, achieving this greener future is not the responsibility of digital health technology developers alone. It requires the active involvement of health systems in implementing these technologies, managing electronic waste responsibly, transitioning to paperless operations, and educating their staff and patients about the environmental impact of health care.

Moreover, the journey to zero emissions necessitates a shift in mindset. It requires viewing the health of individuals, communities, and the planet as interconnected, understanding that we cannot sustain one without the other. It demands we view technology not as an end in itself but as a tool to create a health care system that is not only more efficient and effective but also more sustainable. In essence, digital health's journey to zero emissions is a pursuit of dual sustainability—sustaining human health while sustaining our planet. As we continue on this journey, let us carry forward the insights and lessons from this chapter, committed to harnessing the power of digital health technologies for a greener, healthier future for all. As we strive for perfect health care, let's remember that perfection lies not just in curing disease but in doing so in a way that nurtures the world we all share.

ZERO MISTRUST

DR. ROBERTS IS a seasoned physician who prides himself on his ability to connect personally with his patients. When the medical group he works for decides to implement a new digital health technology, a comprehensive electronic health record (EHR) system with integrated AI-based diagnostic tools, he is apprehensive.

Mary, one of Dr. Roberts's longtime patients, is also unsure about the new system. She values the personal interaction she has with Dr. Roberts and fears that the digital transformation will impersonalize her health care experience.

In the early stages of using the new EHR system, Dr. Roberts encounters a case where the AI diagnostic tool suggests a different diagnosis than his own based on a patient's symptoms and health records. The difference in opinion leads to confusion and uncertainty. As a result, he loses confidence in the technology, leading to a mistrust in the system's reliability.

Simultaneously, Mary begins experiencing issues with the patient portal of the new system. She finds the data usage policies difficult to understand and is unsure how her information is being used or who has access to it. She also experiences technical glitches while trying to schedule appointments and access her health records, leading to a sense of frustration and mistrust.

After several such incidents, both Dr. Roberts and Mary become skeptical of the new technology. Dr. Roberts feels that the technology undermines his medical expertise, and Mary feels her privacy is potentially compromised and misses the human touch in her care.

As we delve into another integral chapter of our journey toward perfect health care, we confront an issue that, while not new, has taken on new dimensions in the digital age: mistrust. In the era of digital health technology, trust remains a crucial pillar, significantly influencing the acceptance and effective utilization of these innovations, as illustrated in the case of Dr. Roberts and Mary.

While digital health technology promises transformative changes in health care delivery, from personalized medicine to remote patient monitoring, its adoption is not without challenges. Perhaps one of the most profound of these is the issue of mistrust. This mistrust can emanate from a variety of sources: concerns about data privacy and security, fear of depersonalized care, uncertainty about technology's effectiveness, and apprehension toward algorithmic bias, to name a few.

Further, mistrust isn't confined to patients. Health care providers too may harbor doubts and reservations toward digital health technology, stemming from concerns about workflow disruption, reliability of digital tools, potential malpractice risks, and the perceived threat to their professional autonomy.

In this chapter, we will delve into these facets of mistrust in the context of digital health technology. We will navigate the intricate landscape of trust and mistrust, exploring the concerns and fears from both patient and provider perspectives, and scrutinize their underlying causes. In doing so, we'll identify potential strategies for trust-building, shedding light on the steps that health care systems, digital health technology developers, and policymakers can take to bridge this trust gap.

The journey toward perfect health care necessitates not just technological advancements but also a deep understanding and mitigation of the barriers to its adoption. As we start this chapter, we realize that the path to zero mistrust is both challenging and imperative. Our goal is to comprehend and address these issues of mistrust, crafting a future where digital health technology is not just advanced but also trusted, thereby enabling a seamless transition toward the health care of tomorrow.

Trust is a critical element of the patient-physician relationship and the broader health care system. With the advent of digital health technologies, this traditional relationship is undergoing a transformation, bringing along new complexities of trust or mistrust. Mistrust can have significant consequences for both patients and physicians, affecting the adoption, implementation, and overall efficacy of digital health technologies. For patients to accept and adhere to treatments, and for physicians to confidently administer care, a foundational layer of trust must exist.

For patients, mistrust of digital health technology can have a number of negative consequences, including the following:

- inhibited adoption. Mistrust in digital health technologies can lead to lower adoption rates among patients. Concerns about data privacy, security, and the reliability of digital tools can deter patients from using them, even when these technologies could offer significant health benefits.
- reduced engagement. Even if patients adopt digital health technologies, mistrust can lead to low engagement levels. If patients do not trust the technology or the organization behind it, they may not use it to its full potential, diminishing the technology's effectiveness. This can be especially harmful for patients who live in rural areas or who have difficulty accessing traditional health care providers.
- health risks. Mistrust can result in patients avoiding or ignoring the health recommendations derived from digital health technologies. This can lead to missed opportunities for early diagnosis, delay in treatment, and ultimately poorer health outcomes.
- lower quality of care. When patients mistrust digital health technology, they may be less likely to share their data with their health care providers. This can make it difficult for providers to provide the best possible care.
- increased costs. Patients who mistrust digital health technology may be more likely to use traditional methods of care, which can increase costs. For example, patients who mistrust telehealth may be more likely to travel to see a doctor in person, which can be costly.

- misinformation and disbelief. Patients who mistrust the health care system may be more susceptible to health misinformation and less likely to believe accurate information provided by health care professionals or public health authorities.

For physicians, mistrust of digital health technology can also have a number of negative consequences, including the following:

- resistance to Integration. Physicians might resist integrating digital health technologies into their practice due to mistrust. This can stem from concerns about technology's impact on their workflow, the reliability of the tools, or fear of losing professional autonomy.
- decreased efficiency. If physicians do not trust a digital tool, they may double-check its outputs or avoid using it altogether, leading to decreased efficiency and potential delays in patient care.
- legal and ethical concerns. Physicians may worry about potential legal and ethical implications of using digital health technologies, such as liability for malpractice in the event of a technology failure or algorithmic bias.
- reduced innovation. When patients mistrust digital health technology, it can discourage innovation in the health care industry. This can prevent the development of new and better ways to care for patients.

Understanding how digital technologies might negatively impact trust from both patient and provider perspectives is crucial in designing digital health interventions that promote rather than hinder trust.

For Patients

- Data privacy and security. With the rise of digital health technologies, the amount of personal health information

collected and stored has increased exponentially. They worry that their data could be used to track them, target them with advertising, or even be used against them in court. The fear of data breaches or misuse of personal health data is a significant driver of mistrust among patients.
- Lack of transparency. Often, patients do not fully understand how their data is being used or how the technology works. This lack of transparency can foster suspicion and mistrust.
- Depersonalization of care. Some patients may fear that digital health technologies could lead to impersonal care, where technology replaces the human touch. They may worry that the empathetic connection between them and their health care provider may diminish, leading to mistrust.
- Lack of understanding. Many patients do not understand how digital health technologies work. This can make them feel uneasy about using these technologies, especially when they are asked to share their personal data.
- Uncertainty about effectiveness. Doubts about the accuracy and reliability of digital health technologies can also lead to mistrust. Patients may question whether these technologies can truly match or exceed the standard of care they receive in person.

For Physicians

- Workflow disruption. Physicians often worry that digital health technologies will disrupt their existing workflows, adding more to their workload rather than easing it. This potential disruption can create mistrust and resistance to adoption.
- Reliability concerns. Like patients, physicians may also question the accuracy and reliability of digital health technologies. There is still a lack of evidence on the effectiveness of many digital health technologies. This makes it difficult for physicians to know whether or not these technologies are safe and effective.

They may be concerned about potential malfunctions or errors that could adversely affect patient care.
- Professional autonomy. Some physicians may perceive digital health technologies as an intrusion into their professional autonomy. They might worry that algorithms could replace their clinical judgment, leading to mistrust.
- Legal and ethical implications. The possible legal and ethical implications of using digital health technologies can also cause mistrust among physicians. Concerns about liability, potential bias in algorithms, and the impact on the patient-physician relationship are among the key issues.
- Cost. Digital health technologies can be expensive, both for patients and for health care providers. This can make it difficult for physicians to justify the use of these technologies, especially when there is a lack of evidence on their effectiveness.

As digital health technologies continue to proliferate, understanding and mitigating the factors contributing to mistrust becomes an imperative task. By addressing these concerns, we can foster a climate of trust, facilitating the adoption and effective utilization of these transformative technologies. In this context, the roles of digital technology developers and health care systems are pivotal.

Role of Digital Technology Developers

- Enhancing data security. Developers must prioritize robust security measures to protect patient data. By leveraging advanced encryption technologies, incorporating stringent access controls, and regularly testing and updating these measures, they can alleviate concerns about data privacy and security.
- Increasing transparency. Developers can mitigate mistrust by making their technologies more transparent. This could involve explaining how data is collected, stored, and used or elucidating

how their algorithms work, making it clear that they are tools designed to aid, not replace, human health care providers.
- Ensuring accuracy and reliability. Developers need to rigorously test their technologies to ensure accuracy and reliability. By demonstrating that their products have undergone extensive testing and validation, they can address concerns about effectiveness and reliability.
- Making digital health technology accessible to everyone. Digital technology developers should make digital health technology accessible to everyone. This includes providing affordable devices and services and making sure that technology is accessible to people with disabilities.
- User-centered design. Technologies should be designed with the user in mind. By involving patients and health care providers in the development process, developers can ensure that their technologies are user-friendly, meet the needs of the users, and integrate seamlessly into existing workflows.
- Ensuring that digital health technology is aligned with patient values. Digital health technology should be aligned with patient values. This means that it should be designed to be safe, effective, and respectful of patient privacy.
- Building trust with patients and physicians. Digital technology developers should build trust with patients and physicians by being open and honest about the benefits and risks of their products and services. They should also answer any questions that patients and physicians have and be supportive of patients and physicians who use their products and services.

Role of Health Care Systems

- Education and training. Health care systems can play a vital role in mitigating mistrust by educating both patients and health care providers about the benefits and limitations of digital

health technologies, their use, and their impact on health care delivery.
- Policies and guidelines. Implementing clear policies and guidelines can help address legal and ethical concerns. These policies should clarify issues such as liability, data ownership, and the use of digital health technologies within the patient-physician relationship.
- Promoting patient-centered care. Despite the increased use of technology, health care systems must continue to emphasize the importance of patient-centered care. Digital health technologies should complement, not replace, the personal connection between patients and health care providers.
- Making digital health technology available to patients. Health systems should make digital health technology available to patients. They should address the digital divide by making digital health technology accessible to everyone, regardless of their income or location. This includes providing access to devices and services as well as support for patients who use digital health technology.
- Promoting patient engagement. Health systems should promote patient engagement in the use of digital health technology. This includes providing patients with the opportunity to learn about digital health technology and to share their experiences with it.
- Showcasing success stories. By sharing positive outcomes and experiences related to the use of digital health technologies, health care systems can demonstrate their effectiveness and reliability, building trust among patients and providers.

Additionally, regulating digital health technology is crucial. Governments should regulate digital health technology to ensure that it is safe, effective, and fair. Regulation can help to protect patients from harm and to ensure that digital health technology is used in a responsible way.

Addressing mistrust in digital health technologies requires a multifaceted approach involving digital technology developers, health care systems, and policymakers. By prioritizing data security, enhancing transparency, focusing on user-centered design, and promoting education, policy development, and patient-centered care, we can pave the way for greater trust in digital health technologies. This will enable us to fully harness their potential in transforming health care delivery, leading us closer to our goal of perfect health care.

As we conclude this chapter, it becomes evident that mistrust is a significant barrier in the path toward the full realization of digital health technologies' potential. It's clear that these tools, although transformative in their capability to refine and revolutionize health care, must navigate the complex terrain of trust to be truly effective and widespread.

The journey toward zero mistrust is not a solitary quest for technology developers or health care providers but a collective effort necessitating a balance of advancements in technology and upholding the sanctity of the patient-physician relationship. From enhancing data security, increasing transparency, incorporating user-centered design to providing education, implementing robust policies, and upholding patient-centered care, a multitude of strategies must converge to diminish mistrust. As digital health solutions continue to evolve, they will become more and more transparent, secure, and accessible. Additionally, as governments and regulators develop frameworks for governing digital health technology, we can expect to see even greater trust in this technology.

However, it's critical to remember that while the destination is zero mistrust, the journey itself is of equal, if not more, importance. It is through this journey that health care providers, patients, and technology developers engage, learn, innovate, and grow. As we proceed, we should continually evaluate and learn from our experiences, making necessary adjustments to foster an environment of trust in this digital age.

Ultimately, the road to zero mistrust isn't a direct or straightforward path but a dynamic, evolving process that mirrors the transformative and innovative spirit of digital health itself. Achieving zero mistrust would mean a world where digital health technologies are not just tools but trusted allies in our pursuit of better health outcomes, enhanced patient experiences, and a more efficient health care system. As we look forward, we see not just challenges to be solved but opportunities for growth, improvement, and the realization of the ultimate quest of perfect health care.

ZERO PROMISE SCORECARD

THE HEALTH CARE landscape is undergoing rapid digital transformation, driven by advances in technology and the increasing need for efficient and personalized care. Amid this, the "Zero Promise Scorecard" stands as an essential tool for assessing digital health technologies' impact on the health care industry. The scorecard presents a set of aspirational goals, referred to as the "seven zeros": zero cost care, zero harm, zero wait, zero stage, zero excluded, zero mistrust, and zero emission.

The "Zero Promise Scorecard" directly aligns with the global objective of universal health coverage. The goal of zero excluded, for instance, ensures that digital health technologies cater to everyone, irrespective of their socioeconomic status, language, digital literacy, or geographical location. Aspiring to this goal encourages companies to develop solutions that increase health care accessibility, hence fulfilling their societal responsibilities and earning trust from consumers and stakeholders.

Secondly, a good score on the zero harm and zero stage categories can position a company as a leader in patient safety and early disease detection. Striving for these goals encourages the development of products that prioritize patient safety and enable early intervention, thus driving better health outcomes. These attributes can differentiate a company in a crowded market, attract partnerships, and establish a reputation for delivering high-quality care.

The zero cost care criterion encourages digital health companies to create affordable solutions, which is crucial in an era where rising health care costs are a major global concern. By striving for this goal, companies not only make health care more affordable but also increase their potential market reach, which can translate into long-term sustainability and growth.

Achieving zero wait involves developing technologies that streamline processes and improve health care efficiency. This is particularly valuable in health care settings where timely intervention can significantly improve patient outcomes. Moreover, efficient services also enhance patient satisfaction, leading to better reviews and higher usage of the technology.

Trust is a cornerstone of health care. The zero mistrust criterion pushes digital health companies to create transparent, reliable, and secure technologies. By doing so, companies can foster patient trust, which is key to technology adoption and long-term success.

Lastly, the zero emission goal encourages digital health companies to adopt environmentally friendly practices. This is increasingly important in today's climate-conscious world, and companies that demonstrate commitment to sustainability can enhance their brand image, appeal to ecoconscious consumers, and meet regulatory standards.

Our "Zero Promise Scorecard" provides a comprehensive framework for digital health companies to assess and improve their technologies. Aspiring to a good score on this scorecard aligns companies with important health care and societal goals, differentiates their products in a competitive market, and fosters trust with consumers and stakeholders. Therefore, it is crucial for digital health companies to strive for these "zeros," not only to succeed in the market but also to contribute meaningfully to the global mission of achieving better health for all. Achieving these lofty goals requires strategic planning, conscientious development, and constant evaluation. Here's how innovators can work toward this aspiration:

zero cost car: Develop cost-effective solutions. This could be achieved by adopting open-source software, optimizing algorithms for efficient processing, or partnering with health care providers to distribute costs. Innovators should also consider integrating with existing health care systems to decrease implementation costs.

zero harm: Prioritize safety and security in the design process. This includes implementing robust data privacy and security measures and providing clear, user-friendly instructions to prevent misuse.

Furthermore, adopt a user-centered design approach to ensure technologies align with the needs and abilities of end users.

zero wait: Emphasize real-time response and fast processing times in the development process. Employ agile methodologies for quicker iterations and improvements, and ensure scalability to handle increased demand without compromising performance. Implement user-friendly interfaces to expedite patient-provider communication.

zero stage: Incorporate predictive analytics, machine learning, and artificial intelligence to detect diseases at the earliest stages. Work closely with medical experts to validate these technologies and ensure they're reliable and accurate.

zero excluded: Ensure solutions are accessible and inclusive. Design for different abilities, age groups, languages, and levels of digital literacy. Also, consider affordability and availability across different regions, including rural or underprivileged areas.

zero mistrust: Be transparent about data usage, privacy policies, and the benefits and limitations of your technology. Involve health care professionals in the development and validation process to increase trust. Regularly seek feedback from users and incorporate it into improvements.

zero emission. Develop solutions that are energy-efficient and environmentally friendly. Consider the life cycle of your product from production to disposal, aiming to minimize its environmental impact. Prioritize sustainable practices in your company's operations.

In addition to these, it's crucial for innovators to collaborate with health care professionals, patients, and regulatory bodies. This promotes understanding of real-world challenges and ensures solutions are medically sound, patient-friendly, and compliant with health care regulations. Finally, innovators should adopt a culture of continuous learning and improvement, staying updated with technological advances and health care trends, and iterating their solutions as needed.

Scorecard Measures

Please rank each statement from 1 (strongly disagree) to 5 (strongly agree). Below are the scales.

Zero Cost Care

$Z = (A + E + R + D + I) / 5$

Where:

Z is the overall ability of the digital health technology to achieve zero cost medicine.

A is the affordability of the technology (can be commoditized and priced in a way that makes it accessible to all).

E is the efficiency of the technology. (Does it reduce costs by streamlining processes, reducing waste, etc.?)

R is the reduction in traditional health care costs. (Does it empower patients to take care of their own health, does it reduce the need for expensive procedures, hospital stays, etc.?)

D is this primarily a smartphone-based digital solution. (The scalability of the technology—can it serve a large number of patients without significantly increasing costs?)

I is the indirect cost savings. (Does it help prevent diseases and conditions that would be expensive to treat?)

Each of these variables could be measured on a scale of 1 to 5, with 1 being very low and 5 being very high. The average of these five variables would give an overall score for the ability of the technology to achieve zero cost medicine.

Zero Harm

$Z = (A + C + D + S + P) / 5$

Where:

Z is the overall ability of the digital health technology to achieve zero harm health care.

A is the accuracy of the technology. (Does it provide accurate information and reduce errors? The technology is supported by evidence? Technology supports safe and effective treatment plans?)

C is the communication facilitated by the technology. (Does it improve communication between health care providers and between providers and patients?)

D is the decision support provided by the technology. (Does it help health care providers make better, safer decisions? The technology enhances diagnostic accuracy?)

S is the safety features of the technology. (Does it have features specifically designed to prevent harm, such as alerts for potential drug interactions? The technology can minimize manual or administrative errors?)

P is the patient/provider centeredness of the technology. (Is it easy to use correctly, and are health care providers well-trained in its use? The technology improves patient monitoring? The technology promotes clear communication between health care providers and patients?)

Each of these variables could be measured on a scale of 1 to 5, with 1 being very low and 5 being very high. The average of these five variables would give an overall score for the ability of the technology to achieve zero harm health care.

Zero Wait

$ZW = (E + S + U + R + A) / 5$

Where:

ZW is the overall ability of the digital health technology to achieve zero wait time or instantaneous access.

E is the efficiency of the technology. (This includes the energy used by devices, servers, and network infrastructure. The technology could reduce the need for in-person visits;

how quickly it can process requests and deliver results.)

S is the scalability of the technology. (Can it handle a large number of simultaneous users without slowing down, is it accessible at all times, and does it facilitate immediate access to care and from all locations?)

U is the usability of the technology. (Is it easy to navigate and does it facilitate quick access to necessary features?)

R is the remote capability of the technology. (The technology provides remote patient monitoring or at-home diagnostics and treatment.)

A is the automation capability of the technology. (Virtual assistants within this technology help patients schedule appointments, refill prescriptions, and answer their questions, which can reduce wait times. The technology enables asynchronous communication between health care providers and patients.)

Each of these variables could be measured on a scale of 1 to 5, with 1 being very low and 5 being very high. The average of these five variables would give an overall score for the ability of the technology to achieve zero wait time or instantaneous access.

Zero Stage

$Z = (P + E + I + C + D) / 5$

Where:

Z is the overall ability of the digital health technology to achieve zero stage medicine.

P is the predictive capability of the technology. (Can it accurately predict health risks based on genetic, lifestyle, and other factors?)

E is the effectiveness of the technology in promoting early detection. (Does it facilitate regular health checks and screenings? Supports proactive disease management?)

I is the influence on behavior change. (Technology engages patients in their health care. Does it effectively encourage healthier lifestyle choices?)

C is the ability of technology to support continuous monitoring of patient health data.

D is the data privacy and security. (Does it protect user data and maintain trust, which is crucial for widespread adoption?)

Each of these variables could be measured on a scale of 1 to 5, with 1 being very low and 5 being very high. The average of these five variables would give an overall score for the ability of the technology to achieve zero stage medicine.

Zero Excluded

$A = (I + A + U + R + E) / 5$

Where:

A is the overall ability of the digital health technology to achieve zero exclusion.

I is the *inclusivity* of the technology. (Does it cater to all demographics, including those with disabilities, the elderly, different languages, etc.?)

A is the *affordability* of the technology. (Is it economically accessible to all, including low-income individuals?)

U is the *usability* of the technology. (Is it user-friendly, easy to understand and use by all, including those with low digital literacy?)

R is the *relevance* of the technology. (The technology supports remote health care delivery. Does it meet the diverse health needs of all individuals?)

E is the equality in distribution and *access*. (Is the technology equally available and accessible in all regions, including rural and remote areas?)

Each of these variables could be measured on a scale of 1 to 5, with 1 being very low and 5 being very high. The average of these five variables would give an overall score for the ability of the technology to achieve zero exclusion.

Zero Emission

Where:
$ZE = (E + R + L + DC + S) / 5$

ZE is the overall ability of the digital health technology to achieve zero emissions.

E is the energy efficiency of the technology. (This includes the energy used by devices, servers, and network infrastructure. The technology is designed with energy efficiency in mind. The technology promotes remote health services.)

R is the use of renewable energy by the technology. (Technologies powered by renewable energy sources, such as wind, solar, or hydroelectric power, have a lower carbon footprint.)

L is the life cycle emissions of the technology. (This includes the emissions produced during the manufacturing, use, and disposal of the technology; technologies that are durable and have a long life span can have lower life cycle emissions than those that need to be replaced frequently).

DC is the data center efficiency.

S is the digital optimization. (The technology reduces the need for physical resources or supports digital documentation.)

Each of these variables can be calculated separately, taking into account the specific circumstances of each factor. For example, E might be calculated based on the device's power rating, its typical usage pattern, and its expected life span. Each of these variables could be measured on a scale of 1 to 5, with 1 being very low and 5 being very high. The average of these five variables would give an overall score for the ability of the technology to achieve zero emissions.

Zero Mistrust

$T = (U + R + S + P + C) / 5$

Where:

T is the *overall trust* in digital health technology.

U is the *usability* of the technology (ease of use, user-friendly interface, easy to use and understand, and it is compatible with existing systems).

R is the *reliability* of the technology (accuracy, consistency, provides accurate and reliable results includes mechanisms for human oversight and intervention, etc.).

S is the *security* of the technology (data privacy, protection against breaches, etc.).

P is the *perceived usefulness* of the technology. (Does it meet the user's needs? Does it provide value?)

C is the *credibility* of the source. (Is the technology from a reputable company or organization? Is it clinically validated?)

Each of these variables could be measured on a scale of 1 to 5, with 1 being very low and 5 being very high. The average of these five variables would give an overall trust score.

Pioneers	Progressives	Promising	Potential
score above 30	score between 20 and 30	score between 10 and 20	score below 10

Pioneers (Score above 30)

Digital health technologies that fall into the pioneers category are true industry trailblazers. They have made significant strides across all variables, embodying what it means to provide quality, timely, inclusive, and environmentally friendly health care. These technologies set a high benchmark, leading the way for others to follow. They have effectively addressed the most significant challenges in health care and are paving the path for a healthier future.

Progressives (Score between 20 and 30)

Falling into the progressives category, these technologies demonstrate substantial advancements in digital health. While they might not lead the pack, they are not far behind, showcasing strong performance across several variables. These technologies are on an upward trajectory, continually evolving and improving, working toward becoming the gold standard in their respective areas.

Promising (Score between 10 and 20)

Digital health technologies in the promising category show considerable potential. While they may not yet excel across all variables, they have made important strides in certain areas and have the foundation necessary for significant future progress. With targeted improvements and innovative leaps, these promising players can grow into powerful changemakers in digital health.

Potential (Score below 10)

The potential category includes digital health technologies that are in their early stages or those needing significant improvements across variables. However, their current score doesn't reflect their potential for growth. With a keen focus on enhancement, the adoption of user feedback, and continued development, these technologies hold the potential to climb the ladder and revolutionize digital health care in the future.

Badges to Recognize Scores of 5 in Any Category

Zero cost care: "altruist." You provide health care services without any financial burden on the patients. It emphasizes the commitment to offering care that is accessible and affordable to all, regardless of their financial situation. This concept could be used as a branding approach for organizations or programs that focus on delivering cost-free health care services (blue/green).

Zero harm: "guardian." A commitment to ensuring patient safety and eliminating harm within health care settings. It highlights the dedication to providing high-quality care that prioritizes patient well-being and minimizes any potential risks or adverse events. This concept could be employed to recognize health care facilities or initiatives that have achieved exceptional standards in patient safety and harm prevention (purple or navy blue).

Zero wait: "time saver." Communicates the commitment to reducing waiting times and optimizing efficiency in health care delivery. It reflects a focus on streamlining processes, enhancing access, and minimizing unnecessary delays. This concept could be utilized as a branding element for health care organizations that prioritize timely and efficient care, emphasizing their dedication to reducing waiting times for patients (orange or yellow).

Zero stage: "the predictors." Ability to identify and predict health conditions at an early stage, enabling proactive interventions and improved outcomes. It conveys a focus on early detection, preventive care, and personalized medicine. This concept could be utilized to recognize health care programs or technologies that excel in predictive analytics, risk assessment, and early disease detection (teal or deep green).

Zero excluded: "inclusion idol." The future of digital health is promising, but its potential can only be fully realized when these technologies are available to all, irrespective of their socioeconomic or demographic backgrounds. The "Inclusion Idol" badge isn't just an award but a reminder and a goal that our mission in digital health is to leave no one behind. The pursuit of zero exclusion in digital health will require continued effort, collaboration, and innovation. As technology continues to evolve, we must ensure that these advancements contribute to a more inclusive and equitable health care future for all (rainbow colors).

Zero mistrust: "trust transformer." Commitment to building trust and transparency within the health care system. It signifies a focus on fostering open communication, ensuring patient confidentiality, and strengthening the bond between health care providers and patients. This concept could be used as a branding approach for organizations that prioritize building trusting relationships and reducing mistrust in health care (light green or soft brown).

Zero emission: "Ecowarrior." Dedication to environmental sustainability and reducing carbon emissions within the health care sector. It highlights the role of health care organizations in combating climate change and promoting ecofriendly practices. This concept could be utilized as a branding element to recognize health care facilities or initiatives that have implemented sustainable strategies and achieved significant reductions in their carbon footprint (green or earthy tones).

The "Zero Promise Scorecard" represents a powerful framework for recognizing achievements in various aspects of health care. These categories and badges symbolize the dedication and progress made toward important goals, such as zero cost care, zero harm, zero wait, zero stage, zero exclusion, zero mistrust, and zero emission. It embodies a commitment to excellence and innovation in various areas of health care. By striving for zero in specific domains, these badges symbolize a dedication to pushing boundaries, improving outcomes, and transforming the health care landscape.

The pioneers represent trailblazers who have already achieved remarkable milestones in their respective areas, setting the standard for excellence and inspiring others to follow suit. They have demonstrated outstanding achievements and serve as role models for the industry.

The progressives have made significant strides toward their goals and continue to make measurable progress. They have embraced innovation and implemented strategies that have led to tangible results, creating positive change and advancing the quality of care.

Promising represents the potential for growth and success. Organizations or technologies labeled as promising show great potential in their respective domains, with the ability to make a significant impact and achieve exceptional results. They may be early-stage initiatives or technologies poised for significant advancements and breakthroughs in the near future.

The potential badge represents those who possess the capabilities and qualities to make a meaningful impact in their respective domains. They have shown promise and dedication, and with continued effort and support, they have the potential to become leaders and catalysts for positive change.

Each badge carries its unique significance, whether it be zero cost care, zero harm, zero wait, zero stage, zero excluded, zero mistrust, or zero emission. These badges highlight specific achievements and excellence in areas critical to the health care industry. They exemplify a commitment to providing accessible, safe, efficient, inclusive, and environmentally sustainable health care while promoting trust, transparency, and patient-centeredness.

By recognizing and celebrating the accomplishments of these badge holders, the health care industry promotes a culture of excellence, innovation, and continuous improvement. These badges inspire others to strive for similar achievements and create a ripple effect of positive transformation throughout the health care ecosystem.

The "Zero Promise Scorecard" and the associated badges not only acknowledge past achievements but also act as motivators and catalysts for future progress. They encourage individuals and organizations to push the boundaries of what is possible, continuously raising the bar for excellence and contributing to the betterment of health care for all.

As we continue on this journey, let us celebrate and recognize those who embody the spirit of being pioneers, progressives, promising, and who have earned the badges that represent their dedication to specific areas of excellence. Together, we can transform health care, advance human health, and create a brighter future for all.

CONCLUSION

AS WE CLOSE this exploration of the profound synergy between digital technology and health care, we reflect upon the transformative journey toward the seven "zeros" in health care. Each zero represents an ambitious but essential aspiration in our pursuit of perfect health, serving as a beacon for innovators, health care professionals, policymakers, and patients. We've ventured into the realms of zero cost care, zero harm, zero wait, zero stage, zero excluded, zero mistrust, and zero emission, each forming a critical component in the quest for perfect health.

We have examined the potential of digital technology to enable zero cost care, ensuring that financial barriers do not preclude anyone from accessing necessary medical services. We've probed into the promise of zero harm, with digital tools that enhance safety and reduce errors in health care delivery. The goal of zero wait was scrutinized, realizing how technology could eliminate delays in diagnosis, treatment, and care coordination.

We looked at zero stage, highlighting the role of digital technology in preventing diseases, even before they manifest. We considered zero excluded, where digital tools can be designed and deployed in an inclusive manner that leaves no one behind. The importance of zero mistrust in digital health technology was explored, stressing on the need for transparency, privacy, and user involvement. Finally, we confronted the environmental impact of our digital progress, seeking ways to achieve zero emission and ensure our health innovations do not harm the planet. Each milestone explored demonstrates a vital shift toward perfection in health. These "zeros" aren't just goals but a testament to the immense possibilities that digital health technologies bring.

Throughout this book, we've not only discovered the potential of digital technology to revolutionize health care but also the inherent challenges that come with it. Mistrust, accessibility, and environmental impact are not simple obstacles but complex issues requiring strategic planning, concerted effort, and consistent action.

Innovators, health care systems, and policymakers must continue to work together to address these challenges. They must prioritize trust-building, user involvement, and ensure digital health solutions are accessible, secure, and environmentally friendly. Only then can we fully harness the potential of digital technology and stride confidently toward the goal of perfect health.

However, the journey does not end with these seven "zeros." As digital technology continues to evolve, so too will our aspirations. New goals will emerge, and our definition of "perfect health" will expand and evolve. The seven "zeros" we have identified in this book serve as a foundation for this continuous pursuit of perfection.

The journey to these seven "zeros" in health care is a testament to the transformative power of digital technology. It is a voyage of optimism, resilience, and unyielding aspiration. As we strive toward these ambitious goals, we carry with us a vision of a world where perfect health is not just a distant ideal but a tangible reality made achievable through the power of digital technology.

The quest for perfect health continues beyond the pages of this book. But we hope that the insights, reflections, and visions shared here will guide you, inspire you, and strengthen your resolve on this journey. Remember every small step toward "zero" is a step toward perfect health—and every step matters.